THE

EXPERIENCES

OF A

GAME PRESERVER.

BY

"DEADFALL," OF "THE FIELD."

LONDON:

HORACE COX, 346, STRAND, W.C.

1868.

INTRODUCTION.

To a sportsman, dry details of facts tending to his instruction in a favourite pursuit are usually acceptable; and this being the case, the conveying of that instruction, by introducing on to the scene persons and things partly the creation of the Author's inventive powers, may appear an anomaly, as sporting subjects are not usually looked upon as pills requiring much gilding.

Writing this little book has been a source of very great amusement to the Author. The events narrated have, in most of the cases, happened within his own knowledge. The keepers and poachers are, generally, portraits. In the case of the latter class a recognition by the individual himself followed the appearance of his name (of course disguised) in the article in the *Field*, where it was introduced. With these few preliminary words the Author confides his unpretending exertions to the notice of an indulgent public.

May, 1868.

CONTENTS.

CHAPTER VI.

CHAPTER VII.

CHAPTER VIII.

CHAPTER IX.

CHAPTER X.

CHAPTER XI.

CHAPTER XVIII.

CHAPTER XIX.

CHAPTER XX.

CHAPTER XXI.

CHAPTER XXII.

CHAPTER XXIII.

CHAPTER XXIV.

THE

EXPERIENCES OF A GAME PRESERVER.

CHAPTER I.

Purchase of Estate—Engaging Keeper—His Name and Description—Wages
"Vermin Money," and House—Kennels—Temperature for Guns and Powder
—Keeper carrying a Gun—Description of Vermin Traps.

AFTER several of the early years of my life passed in the
accumulation of a competence abroad, I determined, while
yet comparatively young and in the enjoyment of a good
constitution, to return to the "old country" and devote myself to
the occupation of a "country gentleman"—which ultimatum had
long been my aim. I look upon it that, to live on your own
estate, surrounded by an attached tenantry, and in friendly com-
panionship with agreeable neighbours of your own condition in life,
is a most enviable state of existence. The pursuit of field sports
—especially in all that relates to shooting and the preservation of
game—had from childhood been my ambition; and I was certain
that if I could not get on well amongst the dependents and
neighbours alluded to, it would be their fault and not mine. I was
perfectly aware that numbers had essayed the same occupation, and
had in some instances failed; but I was convinced that in my
own case I might reasonably look for a different result, and, by my
popularity as a "country squire," carry out the intention of legitimate
preserving in all its details. I argued that, with even moderate
advances towards the prejudices of others, and an open and concilia-
tory manner and disposition, he must be a very cross-grained and

B

ill-conditioned fellow with whom I could not "pull," either as landlord or neighbouring landowner.

My first step naturally was to find an estate suitable to the purpose required, and to my means of investment; and although money can command most things in this world, yet it is not always so *very* easy to meet with *just* the thing you want, especially when purchasing an estate is the question. I could hear of properties in first-rate condition as to the farms, &c., upon them, and game to any extent all ready "to hand;" but these were not a *sine quâ non* in my own views. What I coveted was an estate of a good extent, combining all sorts of land, both cultivated and rough; and if with but little game upon it, so much the better—as my intended occupation was to get up the game myself and take a pride in seeing it increase.

From my previous course of life I had had but little opportunity for studying the habits of English game or English vermin, and I therefore promised myself full employment in getting up a fair show of the former and extinguishing the career of the latter. With this view I determined to secure the services of a first-rate keeper and under-keeper, and under their auspices (or, I should say, those of the head keeper) to achieve success, or "perish in the attempt."

After various inquiries and much corresponding with agents and others, and not arriving at any favourable result during such negotiations, I did at last what I ought to have commenced by doing —and that was *advertising in the "Field."* The second advertisement I put in led me into communication with a gentleman who had for disposal just such an estate as I wanted; and six weeks from the period of taking the course named saw me in possession. The property was situated in a northern county of England, six miles from a market town, and four from a railway station. The extent was two thousand five hundred acres of land, a comfortable house and out-offices, a nice trout-stream, and several ponds. Of these two thousand five hundred acres there were nine hundred of moor, and four hundred of moor that had been planted with "Scotch," but which from some cause or other had not done very well, and

were rather thinly standing. The heath consequently was growing
amongst them as luxuriantly as on the open moor, and the trees
themselves were none of them more than about twelve feet high.
This part of my estate seemed, in fact, just the very place for black-
game. There were, I found, a few on it, but not more than an odd
brood or so. The moor also seemed wretchedly off for grouse. But
I am anticipating. There were also about a hundred acres of hard-
wood plantations, including belts and small detached spinneys. The
timber was chiefly oak, with hazel and birch intermixed, and any
quantity of blackberry-bushes of most promising appearance as
covert for pheasants. I found, however, that cattle had been allowed
to wander in the otherwise most game-like looking woods ; and this,
of course, I resolved to put an immediate stop to. I noticed several
little springs of water in the large wood, and here and there a holly
as large as a fair sized hay-stack. Another plantation of about
forty acres in extent, consisted of larch solely ; and nearly adjoining
to it was another of Scotch and spruce, both kinds being of a very
large size. The remaining part of my domain was plough and grass
land ; and on this property I found myself the owner of seven home-
steads. The estate had the advantage of being surrounded by
well-preserved properties, and only on one side was there any small
freehold. That such existed I soon learnt, however ; and I also was
informed that the owner was a very inaccessible, ill-tempered fellow,
and, the property on which he resided being entailed, there seemed,
from what I could make out, but little prospect of purchasing. I
was told, in fact, that one of my neighbouring squires had been at
him about it time after time, but that no amount of money paid
to the man himself, or the person next entitled to the property,
could bring about a sale. It seemed also that this squire and our
friend had met at the market town, and a good offer having been
imprudently made in the presence of sundry small farmers, it was
indignantly refused, and the proposed purchaser had lost his temper
in consequence, and indulged in a series of " elegant extracts in
prose," which had effectually barred the way to any future
understanding.

B 2

My next step was to find two good keepers; and after sundry
applications from persons seeking that situation—some of whom
evidently thought themselves greater swells than their master,
whoever he might be, and some others who might make fairish
"tenters," but not first-rate keepers—I found a man who seemed
"made on purpose" for me.   He was about forty years of age,
unmarried, about five feet eleven in height, and powerfully built.
about the chest and legs.   He was also a very civil-spoken man,
and had evidently lived in the service of some one who knew
how things ought to be—as indeed turned out to be the fact.
He referred me to his last master, who gave him an excellent
character, and who had parted with him solely on account of
giving up shooting.   When I say that he possessed a perfect
knowledge of his business in all its branches of shooting, trapping,
pheasant-rearing, &c., and that his name was Henry Thornton,
I have sufficiently described him.   Before taking any further steps
in the matter of an under-keeper, I determined to consult Thornton
when he had got fully installed into his situation.   There was
one very great point I soon found in Thornton's character, and
that was the fact of his never, in the slightest degree, *presuming,*
if you conversed with him ever so familiarly; and this I was
particularly pleased to find, because there are some men of his class
who rather "forget themselves" under such circumstances, and
these men are my aversion.   Amongst other good qualities, I also
found that he never went into public-houses, or made intimacies
with people whom he might by possibility be called upon some day,
in the course of his duty, to prosecute for poaching; and, although
this might by some be thought evidence of an ascetic disposition,
no such reproach could attach in his case.   I have since got to
know, and have heard of several keepers possessing this peculiarity
(if such it may be called), but who have not, through the course of
conduct named, ever established a character for moroseness or
unfriendliness amongst their neighbours.

The next question was that of wages, which I fixed at 16s. a
week, with a cottage and garden ; and in case Thornton suited me

I held out prospects of a rise in his wages.   I also agreed to give him "vermin money."   This was a novelty to him, as he had never before received it at former situations, and it was only his natural keenness that had induced him to declare war *à l'outrance* to every head of vermin he could come across.   The recompense, fixed upon was 6*d.* for cats, polecats, stoats, weasels, and hawks; and 3*d.* for carrion-crows, magpies, jays, and hedgehogs. ' He was to nail the tails of the " ground vermin " and the heads of the " flying" gentry on a board.   In this bargain he had to find his own powder and shot.   Had my estate been very near a town or large village, I question whether I should have allowed the sixpence for cats, as these animals are so very easily enticed ; but trusting to our comparatively remote situation from either town or village, I did not make any exception.   At the end of the quarter Thornton received his money, and the trophies were destroyed.

The gardener who had lived with the previous owner of my property I found occupying a very nice cottage near the top of a brow which commanded a pretty good view of part of the estate. I concluded to let Thornton go into this cottage, and to settle the gardener in a very comfortable one which could be readily impro- vised out of two excellent "loose boxes," under the same roof with the stables ; and I was glad to find the arrangement was agreeable to both keeper and gardener.

I found I should have to build kennels at Thornton's cottage, and so sent word for a mason and a joiner to be at my house the next morning.   In due course they arrived, and I showed them what I wanted doing, and gave directions to them to set a sufficient number of men to work and get it out of hand.   The kennels were in a courtyard, surrounded by a wall three feet high, and on the top of that was paling reaching another five feet.   The pales were three inches wide, with intervals between each of three inches also.   The whole extent inclosed was five yards square.   On one side was a building with a lean-to roof, and a hole at each end for dogs to go in and out.   The furniture for this house was a wooden sofa, ten feet long by three wide, with sides six inches deep.   This sofa was divided into partitions of the same height as the sides, each partition being two feet six wide, and it stood on legs a foot high. The sofa being filled with oat-straw, the dogs could not rob each other, because each bed was divided from the others. I had the kennel-yard paved with a gradual slope to the centre, where was a sough and grating. Fortunately I was able, with but little trouble and expense, to bring a supply of water through a half-inch pipe into a small trough in the kennel-yard and this I look upon as the chief consideration where dogs are kept.

When the cottage was furnished, I went one evening to see how the inmate approved of all the arrangements I had had made for him, and I found Thornton apparently most comfortable; but the room was to me very hot, and I thought that two guns I noticed hanging up over the fireplace would make the same remark could they have been endowed with the power of language. Henry's opinion, however, was, that if guns are built of really well-seasoned wood, they cannot be kept too warm, and a like atmosphere suits powder as long as it is kept closed from the external air. He was undoubtedly right, I am convinced. Very dry guns and extra-dry powder perform so well, that persons trying the difference, in killing, between guns and powder kept in these places, or in only *moderately warm ones*, would hardly recognise them as being the same. He possessed a double, and a very serviceable-looking single.

One of the first questions he had asked on my engaging him was, "if I wished him to carry a gun regularly?" I was unable to answer this question from my own experience, as I never had previously possessed a landed property, and consequently knew nothing of the requirements of a keeper. I fear I made a blundering sort of reply, and began by quoting what I had read in "Hawker," "Daniel," "St. John," and others. He heard my objections thus obtained at second-hand, and very respectfully suggested that his was a most responsible post; that he took the greatest interest in producing a fair show of game, and although he might be able through the agency of traps and poison to get down the vermin that must inevitably invade my property when the game

began to increase, yet there would be occasions when such devices
would be futile, especially among the large hawk tribe. I was not
in fact prepared to argue the matter, and I willingly left it to him.

I ordered by his directions two score of good bowspring rabbit-
traps—the sort usually sold under this name being large enough
for every sort of ground-vermin ; and I also directed half a dozen
of the round hawk-traps to be sent. "Dead-falls" and "figure
of four" traps I told him to get made according to his own plans
and devices. He suggested that I should get a few different-
priced rabbit-traps sent as specimens ; and three or four kinds of
that make having arrived in due course, he selected those with
the jaws made very light (*stamped out* of the bar of iron), and
not measuring across the jaws, when closed, more than three-
quarters of an inch. Some were sent to be looked at which had
the catch and corresponding notch-piece made of brass, but they
were more expensive, and Thornton told me the others were
equally durable, with common attention and care. I let him get
spikes at the blacksmith's ; and as to chains, I got a long piece sent
by the same people who furnished the traps, and had it cut into
lengths of eighteen inches, and fastened to the traps with "S" hooks.

I had now got things a little into shape, and so determined to
take a walk round every acre of my property, make the acquaintance of my tenants, and master every detail connected with it and
them ; and, should I *fall in* with the freeholder previously alluded
to, I trusted to good fortune at all events not to *fall out* with him.

CHAPTER II.

Inspection of Estate—Sheep Curs—Cottage of a " Gun Man "—Description of Shooting Coat and Gun—Moor—Wadding used by Poacher—Visit to a " Freeholder."

AFTER breakfast next morning I sallied forth in company with Thornton, and called at the houses of several of my tenants. At one I found a couple of snarling ill-conditioned sheep curs, that seemed to me to be far too close a cross with a coarse greyhound or " snap" to be other than dangerous neighbours to my hares when I should have got a few up; but as I had resolved to bring about any reforms that might be needed *gradually*, I said nothing then to the owner. I had on first sight a bad impression of these two dogs, as, instead of greeting us boldly with a good honest bark, they went sneaking off as if they had done something wrong, and occasionally stopped and turned round and " delivered their fire " like skirmishers retiring.

On arriving at a small holding adjoining the moor, I found the tenant's son at home, sitting by the fire in his shirt sleeves. An old and very capacious velveteen shooting-jacket was hanging on the corner of the half-opened door of a pantry, and I was rather amused with this specimen of the handiwork of the country tailor, who appeared to have cut the coat with one side longer than the other, the longest side coming down to a point, and giving the coat a most unfashionable appearance. The owner was a well-built young fellow, but I cannot say that he possessed a very open countenance; he blushed a good deal when we came in, and seemed rather nervous, and rising from his seat, he put a knife and plate into the pantry. Thornton, meanwhile, was unobservedly taking in every little detail, as will be hereafter apparent.

I noticed an old gun hanging to one of the beams by a couple of leather straps, and having a great fondness for guns, and especially old and quaint-looking ones, I took it down to examine it. Originally it had been a flint gun, but was now altered to percussion, yet still possessed its ancient embellishments of brass heel-plate, nose-cap, trigger-guard, and ramrod-pipe. Of this latter appendage there was but *one*. When I had looked it over, Thornton took the gun into his hands, and, after an apparently careless glance at the lock and ramrod-pipe, hung it up again.

Just as the gun was being returned to its place, the young fellow's father came in, and he remarked, "Yes, sir, it's a queer old gun, and not up to much; but it does very well to shoot a rat at the swill-tub, and I got a terrible big 'un the other day. I fancy he was about the last on 'em, for I haven't seen one for better nor a three week."

I happened just then to see the "bolt" lying on the ground; it had evidently slipped out while we were examining the gun, so I picked it up and replaced it.

Hanging to a nail in front of one of the dresser-shelves was the printed bill of a cattle sale, with a piece torn off the foot of it. This bill set us at once on the subject of farming and farming stock in general; and I found that the father had been to this sale, and had only just returned.

Having wished them "Good morning," we continued our walk, and took the road to the moor, one of the boundaries of which was a lane dividing it from a series of pasture-fields. We had gone but a few hundred yards, when Thornton suddenly stopped, apparently with the object of tying his boot-lace, and went rather elaborately through the action of fastening it. On rising, he picked up a piece of paper, crumpled it in his hand, and walked on without saying a word or turning his head.

We went on to the top of the hill, and when we were out of sight of the cottage we had just left, he said "Now, sir, I have found out all about it. I did not like the look of that man's son, nor himself either, for a matter of that. Did you notice the corner of that shooting-coat dipping down to a point?"

" Yes," I said, "I certainly did; but what of that?"

" Why, that was caused, sir, by constantly carrying a gun-barrel in it; and you might have observed (but if you did not, I did) that it was in the *left* side of the coat. The gun was not in it *then*, because the coat swung so light against the door as he opened and shut it when putting those things away in the larder. The gun hanging up is the gun he uses, in spite of that fine story about rats. It hadn't a bit of dust upon it, and the cap was bran new. The barrel was covered with scratches for at least a foot down from the muzzle, and the ramrod-pipe was dented round the front of the edge by thrusting through holes in walls. The gun had been six or eight inches longer in the barrel some day or other, but had been cut short so as to be handy to put in a pocket; and it had not been thought worth the expense of brazing the pipe on again, as *one* had been considered enough. The bolt dropped out from constant wear in taking the gun to pieces. I did not say anything to you, sir, as we came up the lane, but I noticed on the opposite wall to the moor-wall there were small holes pulled just below the coping. I counted thirteen altogether. I daren't call your attention to them, sir, because I could see out of the corner of my eye that the son was leaning over his yard-wall watching us off—though he doesn't know I saw him. When I stopped to tie my boot, as you thought, I picked up this."

Thornton now produced his bit of paper. It was blackened, and very ragged round the edges, but the printed characters, " —mson, Printer, Stanton," were clear enough.

"Now, sir," said Henry, "you might, perhaps, have noticed that a corner of that cattle-sale bill was wanting, and that it was torn off, leaving the words 'Alfred Willia—' printed on it. The rest of that bill you now see. I can show you also, sir, no end of places where a charge of shot has struck the copings of the wall next the moor—and, by the bye, there's one!"

Surely enough there were, at the spot he pointed to, indubitable signs of the gunnery in question having been carried out; and we had not gone many yards before we found it repeated.

"As to the old fellow not having fired a shot for three weeks, as he said, that is not true, for the date of the bill in the left corner was September 16, and to-day is the 24th, so *that* gun must have been loaded and this very shot fired between those two days. Now he knows there's a keeper on the ground, he'll be tolerably careful; but I'm safe to nail him, as I know he can't hold off taking a shot at a grouse."

I need not say how very much interested I was by all this, and I was mentally in admiration of Thornton's Indian-like cleverness.

A walk of a few hundred yards farther brought us to a cross-road. A good-looking young man was sitting on a stone at the turn of the lane, and on our approach he got up and touched his hat to me, remarking that it was a fine day. We stopped to talk with him, and I found that his name was George Oakes, and that he was the son of one of my tenants. He was waiting for his father, who had gone to the cattle-sale.

During a break in our conversation he remarked to Thornton that " a stoat had crossed the gateway going into the sand-quarry ;" and he also informed us that some gipsies who were encamped at the quarry in question had a "'nation likely-looking dog" with them.

As he seemed an intelligent, nice sort of fellow, and evidently rather fond of " keepering," it occurred to me that this was the very man I wanted as an under-keeper, and I resolved to speak to Thornton about engaging him.

Oakes having been informed by myself that I was on a tour of inspection of the estates, asked if I had called at Scourfield's—the name of the tenants I had just left, and at whose cottage I had seen the gun. I told him that I had.

"Ah," he said, " that young Dick Scourfield is a bit of a gun-man."

This remark was just setting me off in the openness of my heart to detail what we had seen, when I was stopped by a very expressive look from Thornton.

Oakes merely went on to say that this man had given Mr.

Reynardson's keepers a great deal of trouble, but that he (Oakes) had himself nearly "nailed" him more than once. I found that Oakes had several times assisted the keepers of my neighbour—in fact, that he had distinguished himself in more than one poaching affair as a coadjutor to the keepers.

The round of visits among my tenantry being concluded, and the inevitable list of dilapidations having been duly hammered into my ears by sundry of the occupiers, I determined to make my way to the residence of our friend, the cross-grained freeholder.

Twenty minutes' walking brought us to his house. He was at home ; and I sent my name in by his wife, who came to the door in answer to my knock. After keeping us waiting nearly five minutes, he at last appeared, but did not ask us in : he lounged against the door-post, and his wife stood behind him, fully prepared to take up the conversation should it get in the least warm, or an invasion of any "rights" be threatened. I commenced the interview by saying, " I have bought the estate here, and as I hope to be on the best of terms with my neighbours, I have called to see you. I trust that we shall be very good friends. I understand that one of your fields runs for 300 or 400 yards into my land. Would you object to myself and keeper, or keepers, making a short cut across it occasionally ? "

This was a bold stroke, and I felt it to be so. It would, perhaps, have been better to let it be for a few weeks before starting such a proposition ; but I had made it, and there was the fact.

" Well," he replied, " you see you and me's not known ought of each other at present. The last feller as owned that property didn't use me well ; he'd always be bothering me to sell, and he'd acterally bid money at the place before half a score of the moorside farmers, and they've chaffed me about it ever sin'. Besides, I gave old Mester Crabbidde's keepers the liberty you wants, and they never sent me so much as a rabbit ; and I knows for a fact that once when one of my ewes was o'ercast and layin' for the whole day on her back, they never touched her, though they must have passed her within ten yards."

I did not, of course, attempt to argue with him upon his so-called *facts;* but I had no doubt in my own mind that his ten yards were a hundred if the truth were known, and that the keepers would have "righted" the ewe in a moment if they had seen her.

Having gradually talked the man into a comparatively good humour, and got him to say "he'd think about it," I left him to digest what I had proposed. It does not do to force *some* people, or to try and "pin them into a corner."

Take it altogether, I was well satisfied with my interview—the more so as his wife had not given an opinion one way or the other; and I am quite sure that one adverse to my interests would have been tendered had she seen an opening, for a more vinegarish-looking lady I had not had the pleasure of seeing for many a day.

CHAPTER III.

Inspection of Plantations—Prints of Vermin in soft Ground—Walls, Gates, and Meuses—Bars of Gates off and Meuses stopped—Finding old Supports for "Hangs"—"Keeper's Tree"—"Dog-wires" in Plantation—Magpies and Carrion-Crows—Covey of Partridges "jugging"—Flock of Sheep apparently frightened—Ascertain Cause—Description of various Kinds of Nets—Keeper's Telescope.

HAVING the best part of the afternoon before us, we determined to devote it to a minute inspection of the plantations, as I was anxious to discover in detail their capabilities for holding game. A little rain had fallen in the night, and it had, in fact, been rather wet for a few weeks previously, and altogether I did not much fancy going amongst trees under the circumstances.

In this matter, however, I had to defer to my keeper, who considered it to be very much in our favour, as, the ground being soft, we should have the better chance of pricking a hare, and also of seeing what marks of vermin there were. We made our way across a very large field of white clover, of a stunted and poor-looking growth, and at the end of this field was my principal plantation. It was the large one, to which I have before alluded; and a more desirable covert could not be imagined.

The clover-field and the fields on each side of it were separated by hedges, but the plantation was inclosed on that side for several hundred yards by a wall of about four feet six inches high. Our first object of inspection was of course *the gate*. It was a very good five-barred one, with oak "head" and "back," and larch bars. To the bars a quantity of upright pales had been nailed, but in one spot a paling was deficient. It had of course been knocked off for the purpose of encouraging hares to go through. The wall was full of "meuses," but not a single one was open—all closed with copings taken off the wall; and it was evident that they had been so closed for several years, as, on removing the stones, we found they had fairly sunk into the ground, and under each were several worms comfortably domiciled.   Not a single tracing of a hare did we see; but there were indubitable marks of weasels and stoats, and also of hedgehogs.   The footprints of the last-named animals I had taken to be those of rats, but Thornton said they were made by hedgehogs, and the marks left by the two animals are, in fact, very much alike.   Where the stoats had gone was plain enough, by the impressions being about fifteen inches from each other longitudinally, two inches apart laterally, and a third footprint just behind and between them.

Having my note-book in my pocket I carefully examined the gate and came to the conclusion that the upright palings made it rather too heavy, and even as they were they did not reach high enough, as a hare could readily take the third bar, and after a snow-drift had shown her the way, would no doubt continue the practice.   I therefore made a memorandum to the effect that a piece of galvanised iron wire netting would be the proper treatment for this gate.   The field, constituted as it was, formed a complete "trap" for a feeding hare.

Before entering the wood we looked the hedges over dividing one field from another.   The runs made by hares in former days were still plain enough, although the grass had grown up in them, and in some of these runs we found little pegs about as thick as a pencil, and with a split in the tops.   Thornton soon detected them, and pulled one up, but it was quite decayed and brittle, and so we found were the others.   These pegs had been placed there as supports for hangs or wires; but the age of them told a dismal story of the scarcity of hares.

The gate out of the next field into the cover was also a very good one, and the posts were strong and firm in the ground.   This gate had been secured with palings, but there was the same hiatus as in the one we had just inspected.   I concluded to mortise some extra rails to it, and to render it a tough job for any one to remove them, and therefore duly took down the measurement of length, &c., &c.

On entering the wood, the first object that caught our notice was the "Keeper's Tree," and I stopped nearly half an hour to hear the *al-fresco* lecture on vermin, delivered by Mr. Thornton. He pointed out every kind known, with the exception of foxes. There were the tails of cats by dozens, and the entire bodies of polecats, stoats, and weasels, and the heads of hedgehogs, hawks, carrion-crows, jays, and magpies. The flying vermin had been nailed up, but the bodies had rotted away, leaving the skulls, with a nail driven through, fast to the tree. Every one was shrivelled up and perfectly dry, and some of the stoats and weasels were really very perfect anatomical specimens. The last had been nailed up seven years ago, since which period no preserving had been carried on.

It would be necessary, of course, to get some hares and other game to turn out a breeding stock, and I had several intimate friends at a distance who would, I was sure, give me what I required; and from what Thornton told me of the mode of catching them, I promised myself a good deal of amusement in assisting at the various captures as soon as leave were accorded. Thornton was most anxious to undertake the task. My neighbouring game-preservers had not "called" yet, so I did not look for any help from them, and especially as they might at the best be chary of giving live game to a stranger, although coming among them as a permanent resident.

Before leaving the large wood we looked it cursorily through, and I resolved to adopt a suggestion of Thornton's as to "wiring" it, for the purpose of protecting the hares from being chased by self-hunting dogs, and as affording a gentle reminder to self-hunting trespassers of the human species. I named to Thornton the circumstance of having read of stout wire being tightly stretched from tree to tree and drawn up by screws. Thornton told me he had always adopted the plan, and had commenced by using screws, but he had "hit on a dodge worth two of it." He explained it as follows :

Get some pins made of $\frac{5}{8}$ iron rod, eight inches long, with a circular eye about an inch diameter (formed by merely bending the iron to that shape), and let the other ends be just hammered round the point to give a "lead." Having selected the trees you mean to adopt as "stretching posts," bore in each a hole with an auger, of such size that the pin will drive pretty tight, but not *too* tight. Let them stand out a couple of inches besides the eye. Having procured a good quantity of galvanised wire, about one size thinner then "telegraph wire," insert an end through one of these eyes, and with a short iron bar give the pin a twist or two; then uncoil the roll of wire, and let it reach to the pin in the other tree, and adopt the same course. Two or three turns at each end soon cause the wire to hum like a guitar string. Drive in staples wherever it touches the intermediate trees. It should be about fifteen inches from the ground. If a dog is in pursuit of a hare, the latter goes *under* the wire, of course, and the dog is caught just about the mouth or chest. Should the "pace be good," a tolerably sudden reversal of the dog's action may be immediately observable, and this is followed up by a decided unwillingness to continue the pursuit. In the night, if pheasant-poachers walk with the centre of the shin-bone against the wire, the result is a tremendous volley of "blessings," succeeded by sickness and nausea; and if the wires are tolerably plentiful, and the above-named dose be repeated, it will cause a future disinclination to enter such hallowed ground!

Such was the apparatus proposed by Thornton, and, in accordance with the precept of Captain Cuttle, of glorious memory, I "made a note of it."

I imagined that we should find more traces of vermin than we actually did; but my keeper said that they would come quite soon enough when the game began to get up (or, as he expressed it, "when there was a good weight—pronounced by my friend 'wite'— of game"). Taking our way towards the larch plantation, we saw eleven magpies feeding near it. Those, when put up, flew off and settled promiscuously on the tops of sundry of the trees; there were also two old carrion-crows on the tops of a couple of Scotch firs adjoining the larch wood.

Thornton stated that he would have very little difficulty in settling the whole lot, but that an evening's magpie-shooting was far from being bad diversion, and if I chose he would, the next day, induct me into the mysteries of the sport in question, which I agreed should be duly carried out. The carrion-crows, he said, did not come into the same category, but must be left to his own separate devices.

As we crossed one of the farms a man came to tell me there was a good covey of partridges on his land, and that he hoped no one would take them. He was the more anxious about it as he had seen young Scourfield hanging about; and, although nothing of the kind had ever been proved, yet it was pretty well known that he had a "bird-net," and could use it too; and he had little doubt he was visiting that locality for the purpose of "jugging" the partridges preparatory to a netting exploit. Thornton asked if the covey had been shot at that season; and being told they had not, he did not express much anxiety about them—at all events, for one night—and simply told the farmer to take a walk about the field where they were in the habit of jugging, and put them up, as, unless shot at during the day, partridges go to roost with little or no calling; but if, having settled for the night, they were again roused, they were safe enough. The man promised to do so.

It was now about time to be making homewards, and we were on our way when the keeper asked me to stop a moment, and see what was the cause of three sheep in a distant field suddenly rushing away from a hedge close to them, and go scampering off as if frightened. At the same moment we saw a man's head appear on the other side of the plantation hedge, and I at once dispatched Thornton to see what he was about. He returned in ten minutes to say he had found three men in the wood *professedly* gathering nuts. As they had, however, no dog with them, and nothing in their pockets, he could do no more than threaten them if caught there again. Had it not been for the sudden movement of these sheep, we should never have known of the men. My keeper said he always observed such "signs" very narrowly, and that horses, cows, sheep, and even birds were often the cause of giving the alarm uuder the like circumstances.

I gave Thornton orders to come down to the house in the evening, as I wished to have a long talk with him, and to consult him about sundry things that I should require in connection with preserving the game. He duly made his appearance, and I directed him to be seated. Being equally anxious with himself to procure the live game spoken of, I asked what apparatus (or as he called it "tackle") I should procure?

"Why, sir," he said, "I have got every kind of net that can be used. I have two 'long nets' of sixty yards each, ten 'gate' or 'sheet nets,' and a couple of dozen 'purse nets.' If you go with us when we catch the hares and rabbits you will see how they are used. I have left my running dog at my cousin's in Newcastle, but I will send for him. I took him from three poachers about eighteen months ago, and a topper he is! I never knew a Christian with more sense. He does not require speaking to when he's at work; but you will judge for yourself, sir."

"By all means," I replied; "write and get him over, as I have heard of such dogs, but never yet saw one."

Thornton asked me if I had a telescope. "Oh yes," I said, "here's a capital one," and at the same time produced a fifteen guinea "Dollond" that had sundry eye-pieces which would show every moon that Jupiter ever possessed; an accurate delineation also of Saturn's ring was a joke to what it would do. It went into a mahogony case, and the whole thing did not weigh more than a stone, or measure more than two feet six. I was rather chagrined at Thornton's mode of welcoming the appearance of this redoubtable optical instrument, and at his by no means jumping at my offer to exhibit its nature and properties.

"The telescope I mean, sir," he said "must be such as you can carry about handily. I had one, but some very tidy person, seeing it in my last house, considered it had no business littering about, so walked off with it. I gave 10s. to Salom for it, and I never saw a better glass for a keeper. I have had a good deal of expense in righting matters at home since my old father died, and, to tell you the real truth; sir, I have not been very well able to afford a new one."

I 'at once promised to purchase one of the same kind for both Thornton and myself.

Just then one of my servants came in to say that a sack of flour had been left in the kitchen, and, as the keeper was there, would I let him put it in the bin for them?   As it would be a dusty job, I told him he had better take off his coat and waistcoat, and in doing so something dropped out of his pocket.

CHAPTER IV.

Vermin Calls—Strychnine—Engagement of George Oakes as Under-Keeper—
Magpie Battue in Evening—Fixing spare Bars in Gates—Visit from Arden,
a neighbouring Keeper—Shooting from left Shoulder.

THE article that had fallen from Mr. Thornton's clothing was about
the size of a shilling, and, in fact, I had, at first sight, imagined it
to be one. He picked it up and gave it into my hand with the
following inquiry : " Did you ever see one of these, sir ? " I was
completely puzzled to make out what it could be. The size of the
thing was, as stated, about that of a shilling, and it was made of
German silver, and in shape exactly like the present detestably
disfiguring regulation forage cap for infantry, having a little peak
projecting straight out. It had a small hole through it, and was
hollow.

With the remark, " Allow me, sir," Thornton took it and placed
it lightly between his teeth edgewise, and instantly produced, with
his breath, sounds so closely approaching the squealing of a rabbit,
that had I not seen the performance, it would have induced me
to swear a rabbit was being killed. " This, sir," said he, " is a
weasel-call, and it makes also a call for sparrowhawks in breeding-
time." He now breathed in a rapid jerking kind of way, and it
made the cry of a sparrowhawk to the life. He told me he had got
a wood-pigeon call at his cottage, which he would show me. These
calls had been bought at Simpson's, in Oxford-street, near the
Regent-circus. The weasel call, he said, was eighteenpence, and the
pigeon call four-and-sixpence.

For carrion-crows, magpies, and jays he made an impromptu call
with his fist lightly closed and placed with the side of the thumb
against the lower part of his under lip on the right side, and the
knuckles upwards. By tightening the lips and inhaling the air

through them he produced a most extraordinary sound, which, by opening and shutting the fist in a very small degree, was made exactly to resemble the cry a hare would make if caught in a steel trap. The noise thus produced in the room was really almost deafening. The servant having left the door open, expecting Thornton in the kitchen to help with the flour, allowed ingress to a great tom cat I had, and this gentleman immediately made his appearance, mewing in a hoarse and unearthly manner. I told Thornton to go on calling, and he began to modify the sound so that it appeared like a cat, and not a hare, in the trap. The veritable cat that had just appeared instantly flew at the keeper, and we really thought it would have gone half wild with indignation. Even after Thornton had stopped, the cat remained walking about the room and continuing his horrible noise, so we hunted him out, but it was an hour or two before he had resumed his usual habit, which consisted in dozing before the fire most of the day.

My keeper, having illustrated his power of muscle by lifting the sack of flour, returned to the room, and our conference proceeded. He asked me to get him some strychnine, as he did not think the chemists would sell it to any one they did not know; and a letter from myself to a medical friend in London would be sure to have effect. Fortunately I was able to rank a doctor among my acquaintance, and I duly undertook to procure some. Getting it from such a quarter, too, I was sure to escape being imposed upon by an adulterated article; for this drug being very expensive (about three-pence per grain), it cannot be got genuine from chemists in country towns.

I took the opportunity of asking Thornton what he thought of young Oakes as an under-keeper. Of course he knew no more about him than I did, but he agreed with me in the opinion that he had a very good countenance, and was a "likely" sort of man for the situation, more especially as he had acted temporarily in that capacity, and was fond of it. I determined to go over in the morning to Oakes's farm, and, if possible, engage the services of the son.

After breakfast the next day, I took a walk to his house, and found him in the stack-yard busy unloading the last load of corn. When this operation was concluded, I named the matter to him, and found that both he and his father were quite agreeable to meet my wishes. It was arranged that he should continue to live at home. I inquired particularly as to his habits, whether he was a very early riser, and not given to drinking or "company." Although it was not likely that either Oakes or his father would give me unfavourable answers, yet altogether I was sure it was all right, and I never afterwards found this confidence misplaced.

George was not much of a trapper, but he could soon learn, he said; neither could he shoot very well, as his performances in this line had been confined to taking a shot at a small bird or a mark occasionally, with the gun of one of the neighbouring keepers. He had no gun of his own, his father having always, as he said, set his face against George having one, since it was sure to get him into a mess some day; and it spoke well for the son that he had never pressed the matter, for he was certainly old enough to have a will of his own, even at home.

I gave directions for Oakes to come to the house at five o'clock that afternoon, as I intended him to take part in the invasion of the magpie roost; and I also told him to go round by Thornton's house and deliver a like message to him.

Our nearest carpenter was about a mile off, so I took the way to his shop and made an appointment for him to be at the large wood the next day with a quantity of light bars for the gates, the dimensions to be two inches and a half wide by seven-eighths thick, and the material sound larch.

At five o'clock Thornton and Oakes made their appearance, the former with his double gun. Oakes was duly fitted out with a single gun of mine, and having myself a double, we started off.

We were a little too early, as the magpies had not yet come in; but in about a quarter of an hour I distinctly heard one chatter, although a long way off. As I knew Thornton would understand how to go about it better than myself, I told him to try and get a shot. He requested me to go for a couple of hundred yards into the wood in one direction, Oakes in an opposite one, and both to keep "as still as mice." He himself ran lightly towards the spot where the magpie apparently was, and when he got within thirty yards of the place he stopped. In a minute or so she gave another chatter, and that same instant Thornton moved quietly on again. This was repeated, and then I saw him raise his gun and fire. A chorus of magpies' voices was instantly raised, and bang went another shot. The flock of magpies then seemed to shift away from him, judging by their noise, upon which he began "calling," as shown to me the evening before. This set every magpie chattering more violently than before. There must have been fifty of them at least. Before the calling had been continued ten seconds, bang! went the gun again, followed instantly by the second barrel at one going over his head, which, after a pause, came brushing through the trees and fell dead close to where I was. The flock now seemed to disperse, and from a movement Thornton made with his hand to Oakes and myself I saw that he wanted us to follow them, which we at once did, he himself remaining on the original spot and "calling."

Going very quietly, I soon got a shot, but only wounded the magpie, which hung in the tree, shouting out fifty thousand murders. Some of its friends at once came to it, to be informed of the worst, whereupon I immediately floored another. They then flew away, but by following them about we kept picking them off to a great extent, as they did not seem to dream of leaving the larch plantation. One of the magpies effectually bothered me. It was in this way: I was certain I had got within ten yards of the tree he was on, but for the life of me I could not see him; I heard him chattering, and that was all. At last I moved a little, and I suppose he caught a glimpse of me, for away he went, and I did not shoot at him. I noticed that Thornton took a shot off the left shoulder once, but I could not quite see for what reason. The magpies being now reduced to a dead silence—not one would speak—Oakes and I joined the head keeper, and we proceeded to "count up." Thornton had got eleven, I had seven, and Oakes seven also. This was a pretty good evening's work; and really I thought it as excellent a piece of diversion in the shooting way as could be hit upon, and suggested that we should repeat the performance next evening. Here, however, I was met by a respectful negative on the part of my keeper, who said that he had proposed it as not calculated to do any harm once in a way, especially as there was little or no game to frighten; but, unless I particularly wished it, he would rather not have another battue of the kind, on account of the disturbance from so much noise of guns. Of course I at once fell in with his views. He told me that he was not fond of too much shooting work, although he always liked to have a gun with him in case of necessity.

During our absence a messenger had brought a note from the station saying that there was a large roll of wire and a heavy parcel for me if I could make it convenient to send over for them in the morning. I gave directions to Oakes to take the spring cart and fetch them away. He got back by nine o'clock, and I had the wires sent down to the large plantation, where I had fixed to meet a carpenter; and after breakfast I went to the locality in question and found the man waiting for me, and Thornton also.

By directions of the latter the gate was taken off its hinges and reared up on end. A mortise was cut in the gate "back," between each of the three lower bars, and then the gate being reversed, the same operation was performed in the "head." For the first-named part the mortise was an inch deep, and in the other half an inch only. Having cut the spare bars an inch longer than the whole inside measure between head and back, one end was driven into the deep mortise, and with a strong mortising chisel it was prised forwards into the shallow one, and then nailed to the upright and slanting support of the gate.

At another gate, which I have described as not being calculated for much increased weight, I had the wire netting fastened on with staples. Oakes knew the different gates on the property perfectly, so I dispatched him along with the carpenter to complete them as we had done these two, leaving it to him to do them with bars or wire net as he might think well.

I had previously told Thornton to get the iron pins he mentioned properly made at the blacksmith's. The carpenter left us an axe, a saw, and a hammer; and I also reserved a good quantity of the small staples. Thornton and I then proceeded to put down the "dog-wires," and in three hours had done about twenty. The pins were placed in the trees on the side diametrically opposite the wire, and the friction of the wire against the half of the trunk of the tree was prevented by the irons being bent when the wire got tight with being screwed up. Where it happened that we had not an intermediate tree handy for staples we cut small posts, about a yard long and three inches thick, and drove them into the ground to fasten the wire. The staples were not hammered *close up*, or they would not have admitted of the wires being slackened out when we came to beat the woods, in which case the *tight* wire might, and no doubt would, injure our own retrievers.

While we were employed, a fine-looking keeper-like man came up and touched his hat to me, introducing himself as Arden, keeper to Lord Charles Mordaunt. He said his master had sent his compliments, and hoped to have the pleasure of calling in a day or two; and, hearing that I was anxious to preserve the game on my property, wished his keeper to afford me any assistance in his power.

This was a good beginning, and I thought that he and Thornton would be just the men to suit each other as neighbouring keepers— *a very great point.*

Arden particularly admired our handiwork, and said he had never seen the plan before, and should certainly adopt it. He had some "pitfalls" in two of their woods, in which poachers had been taken, but they were troublesome affairs to construct. Thornton knew all about such things, and would describe them, and if I wished, would get them made, but suggested that we should try the wires first.

Arden having returned home, and being inclined myself to rest a while, I asked Thornton why he had changed from the right to the left shoulder in shooting one of those magpies.

" The reason, sir, was this: in such work as we were after, you must not be moving about. That magpie, first of all, settled on a tree to my left, but without having observed me she shifted to one on the right. To shoot off the right shoulder I must have turned completely round, and she would have caught sight of me in the movement. By quietly changing the gun to my left hand there was nothing to attract her attention. It is very useful to be able to shoot off the left shoulder, as I have often found, when waiting of an evening at a woodside to shoot rabbits coming out to feed; and, in fact, I can make an *easy* running shot in that way through practice."

I then named to him how that other magpie had escaped.

" You will often find this to be the case, sir," he replied. " You should follow up the perpendicular line of the stem of every larch about the place where you think she is, and by this means you will, in nine cases out of ten, detect her, when you might have looked in vain in any other way."

Having thus explained himself, I proposed that we should go on with our wiring; and, having completed it as far as our supply of wire would allow, we next proceeded to render the meuses secure.

CHAPTER V.

Securing Meuses in Walls—Keeper's "Running-Dog"—Offer of live Hares by
Mr. Long—Description of Nets and Apparatus—A Night's Long-Netting—
Performances of Dog—"Gate" Netting—Meuse or "Purse" Nets—Netting
without Dog.

THE wall in which these had been constructed was, as before stated,
four feet six inches high, and consequently a hare, if *closely* pursued
by a dog, might be caught if compelled to *leap* the wall. The
distance from this fence to the nearest trees in the wood was six
yards, and a long net could be set on the other side with the greatest
ease, as the ground consisted of smooth turf. To finish out the
afternoon, we proceeded to cut down a few young ash and beech
trees, and kept the longest for rails, and cut the shorter ones into
posts about two feet six long. To secure the meuses, one end of the
rail was thrust into the wall just above the covering of the meuse,
and a post driven into the ground at the other end, leaving it standing about eight or ten inches clear of the surface. The end of the
rail was then nailed to this post, and some of the roughest boughs
we could get were also nailed on the top of the rail. We began this
operation with such materials as we could procure on the spot,
because the keeper wished me to see the idea, but he informed me it
would be best completed with *larch* post and rails. I ordered him
to make inquiries where such were to be had, and procure as many
as he would require. He mentioned a plan that, with my permission,
he would adopt to prevent "long-netting," but it might stand over
till we had procured the hares and rabbits to turn out. He intended
also to strew the space between the rails at the meuses and the
covert with all sorts of brushwood and thorns, as the precautions we
had taken at the wall were only to prevent "purse" and "sheet"
netting.

After we had finished, Thornton accompanied me home, partly for the purpose of carrying the tools, and partly to see if his dog had come. On arriving at the house, I found the redoubtable animal had duly made his appearance, and I proceed to describe him as a very large dog—apparently a cross between a "shepherd" and a "snap." His ears were cut sharp, like a terrier, and he had a "bob" tail. Across the loins he was made quite after the model of a hare. His colour was also just like one, and he had a very wiry stiff coat. He received Thornton's congratulations on his arrival graciously enough, but with no outward marks of delight. He impressed me with the idea that he must have very few real friends amongst his kind, and that his own solemn reflections were his chief resource. For all this, however, I admired the dog, and looked at him with a sort of respect. Thornton patted his head, and assured me he was a "deep old beggar," and "Bob"—for that was his name—has given me many an opportunity of fully confirming my keeper's opinion. I need not say how anxious I was to have him tried ; but having no game of my own to catch, there did not seem to be much chance of an occasion for Bob to show his great mental and physical powers. The very next morning, however, by the greatest good fortune, I received the following note :

My dear Houston,—I have only just heard of your whereabouts, and also of your determination to eclipse everyone with your show of game. Now, I know very well that if you have first-rate woods, &c., you will in time get up the game, but it is a slow process. . As those rascally "Rooshians" have appropriated one of my arms (and, unluckily the *right* one), I have not been able to shoot, and am too old to learn shooting off *the left* shoulder. Altogether I am out of conceit with preserving ; and so, if it will help you at all to start with a few hares and rabbits, why, you can come and help to catch them. I'll give you a good lot of live ones, if you'll leave me all the *dead.* We are not well off for either nets or dogs, and I fancy my fellow is no great hand at using them, if we were ; so come prepared with anything in that way that you possess, and be at my place on Thursday, if you can.—Yours, as ever,　　W. LONG.

Nothing could be better or more *àpropos*, so the next morning saw Thornton and myself at the station, accompanied by Mr. Bob and a sackful of nets of all descriptions. A railway journey of forty-five miles landed us at the nearest station to my friend's house, and there we found a light cart waiting to convey the whole party to our destination. As it was quite early in the day, Mr. Long suggested that we should take a look round the land proposed as the scene of our exploits. Thornton considered it " good killing ground," as it would admit of a " set" whichever way the wind might be. The arrangements were, to have a night's netting *with the dog first*, as those rabbits would have to be killed and sent to the market, and to reserve our *live* take for the next night ; and, in the absence of much success, the next after that.

About nine o'clock in the evening the servant came in to say that Mr. Long's keeper and a helper had come in, and we adjourned, therefore, to the kitchen and arranged our plans. Thornton was to " peg," and Middleton (Mr. Long's keeper) to give out the nets, which latter articles were disposed as follows :—A stick about eighteen inches long, and an inch thick, had been cut with a right-angled projection or hook, standing out six inches at one end. The net had been folded up like a rope, and was strung on a thin stick in rings about a foot and a half in diameter. A small leather strap was passed through the whole of the folds, and then buckled to keep all together. Another part of the apparatus was a pointed iron pin, about a foot long ; at a third of its length down there was a solid projecting piece of iron, some four inches long, which slanted downwards towards the point at an acute angle. The top of this pin was turned into a hook, with the back of its " turn" towards the projection alluded to. Thornton had a series of very small leather loops on the inside of the skirt of his shooting coat, and in each of these loops was a hazel peg about two feet and a half long, and as thick as one's little finger. Each peg was half cut through at an inch from one end, and the half of the wood split off, leaving it flat with a shoulder. The other ends of these pegs were pointed, and just charred in the fire to render them hard and easy to thrust into the ground. The nets, as before stated, were sixty yards long, and their width about five feet. The meshes were two inches and a half square, and along each edge of the

net was a stout string, with a couple of yards to spare at the
ends.

Bob was sitting before the fire wearing an extra-grave appearance
on his countenance, evidently fully aware that he was going on
" active service," and being utterly indifferent to the greetings of
Mr. Long or myself.   Having given the men some bread and cheese
and beer, the whole party started off.   " We've fixed to begin at the
Larch Flats, sir," Middleton said, addressing his master ; " the wind
'ud be rather okkard for the 'Edge,' but we'll try that to-morrow
for the live 'uns as Mr. Houston wants."   So to the Larch Flats we
betook ourselves accordingly.   The plantation alluded to was very
like in situation, and in respect to the fields surrounding it, to my
large wood.   It was fenced in by a wall, and the fields running up
to it were about two hundred yards wide.   Middleton had taken the
precaution to leave the gates open leading into the best of the lot of
fields, so we were able to get on to the ground without the slightest
noise, and without having any climbing to do, which would have had
the effect of rendering ourselves visible to the rabbits out at feed.

The night was everything that could be wished : a little wind
blowing from the fields to the wood, and a fairish show of stars,
and it was about ten o'clock.   Having reached the scene of action,
and turned through the gate half a dozen yards, which brought us
within six feet of the wood, Thornton thrust the iron pin into the
ground (in a slanting direction, so that the cross-piece rested flat),
and a peg about a yard from it.   In ten yards he planted another
peg, and so on.   Middleton having unstrapped the net, and fastened
the top string of it to the hook in the iron pin, gave the bundle of
net (strung as it was on the stick) to his man, and silently but
rapidly followed, giving the string a turn round the top of each peg
as he passed it.   By two little jerks the man knew he had set the
net, and instantly went after Middleton with the second net, which
was got down as a continuation of the first.   We now had 120 yards
set, but there were eighty yards of ground unguarded.   What must
we do with that ?   I did not like to ask any questions, but waited the
result.

The sagacious Mr. Bob had, during all these proceedings, kept close to Thornton, with his nose almost touching the back of the keeper's leg. The very instant the last string of the net was fastened, Bob shot off into the field. His first essay was a rapid quartering of the ground *where there was no net set*, and in half a minute the net was sharply shaken; and this began now to be a matter of constant recurrence, and kept the three men hard at work. I noticed also that Bob occasionally made a tremendous charge, apparently at the net, and then vanished into the darkness again. In about three or four minutes he came to the end where I was, and flung himself on the ground, panting as if his heart would burst. He allowed himself a minute or so, and then bolted off and brought in two more rabbits. After this he came and lay down, and could not be induced to try again. It was as if he had said, "I've got all there are, and it's no use going any more." The total number of slain when we came to count up was twenty-seven, and we decided to have a turn on another part of the property, and catch a hare or two if possible. Middleton said he did not expect to do much, as the place where we were going required four or five men to mind the nets we should set.

Leaving the woodside, we came away down the field and through another field into a grass lane, up which we went about a quarter of a mile. At a gate on the right side of the road, Middleton set a net on two sticks which he had cut in the wood we had just left. The net was about six feet wide and six or seven yards long, and stood about a yard high when supported on the sticks. The remaining half was spread on the ground *towards the gate*. As soon as it was set, Bob flew over the wall, and in half a minute a hare dashed through the gate and into the net. Before she had time to think what a mess she had got into, Thornton was on her, and prevented her from giving more than one cry out. The net was up again in an inconceivably short time, and directly afterwards we heard a rapid approach of feet. It was a hare pursued by Bob. She had come to the gate and turned again, most likely suspecting danger. Another second, and in she dashed! This was all we could get at that spot, so on we went a good way farther, where was a gate, and also a few meuses to let out the water in flood time, as the land lay rather low thereabouts. It was but a narrow field, not more than fifty yards across—and the keepers, having set the sheet-net, proceeded to set some of another kind at the meuses. This net was made like a very elongated landing-net, but large in the opening, with a string through every mesh in the edge. This string passed through a wooden runner, and at the end of it (or, I should say, of the two ends brought together) was a small peg about four inches long. Having opened the purse as wide as it would go, the net was adapted to the meuse, and a couple of tufts of grass pressed into the interstices of the wall, along with two of the meshes, to keep it up. The little peg was stuck into the ground. Mr. Long's keeper whispered that he did not expect to do much at this field, as it did not belong to his master, and he had been in the habit of occasionally setting it in the way we were now doing for the purpose of scaring the hares. We, however, took three hares, and three more jumped the wall close to us, and another we distinctly heard go over one of the cross walls dividing the field from the one next to it.

Having done pretty well in the hare line, we dispatched Mr. Long's under-keeper to the house with them, as a sack rubs their eyes, and brings on an inflammation that is frequently fatal. He was told, therefore, to turn them out into some secure building. He also took Bob with him in a rope, as we should be better without than with him, in capturing the live rabbits at the Larch Flats. By the time we arrived on this ground it was half-past eleven, and we had no time to lose, as the rabbits would be coming in very soon from their "first feed." We got the net down successfully, and the men began beating the ground at once. I thought this would have driven the rabbits away from us, but it was not so ; every rabbit out at feed bolted straight past the men to the plantation, and, in fact, *would not be denied.* From previous directions, Mr. Long and myself occupied ourselves for ten minutes in taking the rabbits out as fast as they struck into the net. Following up

D

Thornton's instructions, I found but little difficulty in doing this, but unless I had been so taught I am sure several would have escaped. The plan, it seems, is to catch hold of the rabbit by the back, close to the loins, with the left hand, and stroke the net away from him with the right, being careful to hold him very tight all the while. In the dark, of course, it is somewhat of a chance getting the right grip at once. We had five ",sets" altogether, and then gave it up, having caught thirty-seven rabbits.

CHAPTER VI.

Rabbits " clapping "—Running Hares into Net—Localities where those caught were turned down—Rabbits also—Scourfield (the Poacher) and Friend—Old Ironstone-getter—Thornton disguised—Poachers shooting Grouse—Calling with a Tobacco Pipe—Figure-of-Four Traps—Mud on Wall —Steel Trap how set.

RETURNING over the same ground, we put up four rabbits that had "clapped." This, I was told, was usual where you have no dog. They will clap down and wait for the danger to pass.

As our evening's work was over, and talking could now do no harm, I asked Middleton why he had not made the gate and meuses secure where we caught our last three hares ; and he told me that the land was the property of a small freeholder, who allowed Mr. Long to shoot over it, but who would not have it preserved in any way, and that he (Middleton) knowing it to be good feeding ground, was in the habit of setting it and running the hares into a net, and shaking them well when so secured. The hares we had taken were fresh-come ones, but those that had leapt the walls were " old stage players " that had " been there before."

I then inquired why his own gates were left unbarred, and the reason he gave me was, that they were out tenting very much, and no one dared come poaching. I thought there was not much sound sense in this, when a little trouble would save all the watching, and I intimated as much to Mr. Long when we were by our-selves. He quite agreed with me, and said that he would have it done should he continue preserving, of which he stood in great doubt.

It now began to rain very hard, and we all got wet through before reaching the house, and the consequence was I caught a bad cold and could not go out the next night ; the keepers, however, did, and increased our stock of hares to seventeen, and nine more rabbits ;

so with this supply we returned joyfully home, the hares being conveyed in flat shallow hampers, and the rabbits in sacks.

In the morning after our journey we looked at our prisoners, and found them all alive and fresh except three rabbits. This was, however, of no great consequence, as we had forty-three left. These, I suggested, should be turned out to shift for themselves; but Thornton said that such a plan would never do. They must, he informed me, be initiated into some strong places, such as rocks, or the burrows of former rabbits. The sand quarry possessed the first of these qualifications, and we had no difficulty at this place in finding them most ample accommodation. The hares were a subject of anxiety to my keeper, as the time of the year was against them—it just happening to be at the "fall of the leaf," when the woods are never quite still, owing to the leaves rustling down, at which period the hares would be kept in such continual alarm as to be averse to lying much in them. We could, therefore, think of no better place than the "Black Inclosure" (as I found the piece of planted moor was named), as it was all Scotch fir, and consequently would be free from such disturbance as is caused by the falling leaves in *hard-wood* plantations.

The hares all went off very fairly, but it was evident they had got rather stiff by being confined in the hampers so long.

The telescopes that I had ordered for Thornton and myself had arrived while we were on our live-game expedition, and I wrote for another as a present to Oakes.

The next day, being nearly recovered from my illness, I took a walk by myself to the moor; and, turning out of the footpath leading into the lane close to Scourfield's cottage, I came suddenly upon his son who was leaning over the yard wall talking to another man of his own age or thereabouts. The stranger was dressed in an old velveteen coat and dirty corduroy trousers; he was slightly marked with small-pox, and had dark hair, and a " Newgate frill " under his chin; and he was altogether as ill-looking a rascal as one would wish to see.

I stopped to have (ostensibly) a few minutes' talk with young

Scourfield, but in reality to do a little amateur keepering relative to the *friend*, who, I was sure, was a " bad lot," and one to be *known* when casually seen again.   While we were talking an old decrepit man came up ; he was bent up almost double, and walked painfully with the support of a stick ; his hair was very grey, indeed almost white, and he had a handkerchief tied round his face under his hat ; his dress consisted of a very old smock-frock, and both his trouser-legs were cut up the sides and tied up with string.

On coming close up he asked, in a strong north-country voice, if " ony on us had got ony foire," and at the same time produced a short pipe with tobacco in it. Scourfield fetched a match out of the house, and then I saw that the poor old fellow's left hand was closed, as if it had received an injury, and the fingers were bent into the form assumed when holding a pen. I asked him how he (a powerfully made old fellow as he certainly was) had got to be such a wreck, and he told me it was with working in the ironstone pits. He had had both legs crushed, and his left hand also, and being constantly in the wet, it had induced rheumatism, which had flown to his head and neck.

He asked us the distance to Moor-lane Quarry ; and this being the very one I have previously alluded to, and my own property, I naturally demanded his object in asking. He said he had a sister encamped there, and that she was the wife of a travelling pot-seller. He went on to say, that a keeper whom he had met had told him it was about four miles from the station. I asked, " Whose keeper ? " and he answered, " Hay were a feller as I'd knowed three or four years sin' at Bishop Auckland, and I seed him a couple of hours agone at the station." It occurred to me that the keeper might be Thornton, so I inquired whether he had told him whose keeper he was. " Oh, ah ! " he said, " he were kayper to a man called Hooton or Horton, or summat loike that." " Was it Houston ? " I asked. " Ah, that were it," he replied. " Hay tell'd me hay were going off by the railway till to-morrow night." I gave the poor old fellow sixpence, and told him I could not have either his relation or himself camping on my property. He promised that they should all be cleared off by the next day, if he could influence his brother-in-law, the pot-seller, towards that end.

I did not feel very well, and returned home, and laid up all the day. The next morning, at breakfast, the servant came in to say that Thornton wanted to speak to me, and he was ushered in accordingly. "Why, Thornton," I said, "how is it you are here? I was told you had gone away for the day." "Before I tell you about that, sir," he said, "may I return you your sixpence?" "Return my sixpence!" I exclaimed; "what do you mean?" "Why, sir," he said, "you very kindly gave me one yesterday at Scourfield's cottage." "Why, bless my soul!" I cried; "you must have been the old ironstone-getter." "The very same, sir; and I will now tell you why I appeared before you such a figure. George told me that Dick Scourfield had a mate as came occasionally to see him, and that he was as great a poacher and gun man as Scourfield himself. I had not been gone more than an hour yesterday when I took out the new glass to try it, and happened to look in the direction of their cottage. The two men were trying to catch a sheep, and it struck me that one of them was this poacher. His name is John Randall, and when he is at home he follows greengrocering and has a cart. He's called 'Kettle-hawker' about here. I went home at once, and put those things on, and when I got to the top of the lane I saw you and them two talking, so I nipped round and came up the lane as if from the station, and managed to bring it out about my being off for a day. I knew those fellows would take it all in, and if they meant an early 'call' for a grouse, they would be at it next day. This morning I was laid under the moor wall a good bit before daylight, and as soon as it was beginning to break I heard two men's voices whispering close to me, but on the other side of the wall. Sure enough one of 'em began 'calling,' and in ten seconds an old cock grouse came and settled on the wall. A shot went at him instantly, and he fell off on the moor-side of the wall. He was not killed dead, and so he run a bit. I kept as still as ever, and Kettle-hawker jumped over and began hunting about. He could not find the grouse, and so Scourfield came over too.

Before long the grouse fluttered out of the heath, and both men threw themselves on it. I nipped out and got right on the top of 'em, and fine and soft they looked. Here's the grouse, sir." The whole thing was admirably well done, and the veritable Thornton received a sovereign on the spot, "*vice* the ironstone-getter, who exchanges." Of course I gave directions for summonses to be applied for against both of the scoundrels, and sent a notice to quit to old Scourfield, who, it was well known, encouraged the son in his poaching habits.

Being on the subject of grouse calling, I asked Thornton how it was done, and he told me it was with a bit of new tobacco-pipe about eight inches long, but having the bowl broken off, and that with this instrument, used on the principle of calling magpies, a call exactly similar to that made by a hen grouse is produced. The process is capable of being carried out only while day is breaking; when it gets light, the grouse will not come.

I asked whether any of the new traps had been set, and Thornton told me he had used the insides of the three dead rabbits and part of the bodies also for a lot of the steel traps, and he had cut up the rest of the bodies as bait for some "figure-of-four" traps that he had constructed. He had been anxious to let me know about the grouse shooters, and had not looked at the traps yet, so I proposed to go round with him.

One road lay up a hedge-side leading to the large wood; and in the ditch, not far from where the hedge joined the covert wall, was one of the "figure of fours." The stone was down, and on raising it there appeared the body of a great "hob" stoat. He was so flattened out that his chances of coming "round" again were decidedly remote.

Thornton had plastered some wet earth on the wall of the covert, and made it smooth. The print of a cat's foot was very plain on it. "We have you, my lady," was Mr. Thornton's soliloquy; and sure enough she was in a steel trap a hundred yards on. The trap had been set under the wall, about six inches from it; the spring was parallel with the wall, and the bait hung about a foot or so above the trap. I noticed that bits of mud and grass were stuck in all the interstices about where the bait-peg was, and this the keeper told me was to prevent the mice biting the string and letting the bait fall into the trap. Walls being a great harbour for mice, they can, unless baulked in this way, creep along the peg.

We found another cat in a trap about a couple of hundred yards on ; and our next three figure of fours had each a mouse under the slate. The abundance of mice showed that the weasels and stoats were not very numerous.

Having arrived at the end of the wood, we crossed the corner of a stubble field. About fifty small birds flew up into the hedge, and in the same instant sunk like one bird into it. A hen sparrowhawk had swept over the hedge, but half a second too late. The birds were just safe. Thornton had his single gun under his arm. Like a flash of lightning it was cocked and pitched up to his shoulder. The hawk had then got about forty yards. Bang! "Missed, by Jove!" I shouted as the hawk went on apparently unhurt. "No, sir, he's a dunner!" said Thornton. The hawk suddenly commenced falling and rising, and, at last, went a regular "cropper" into the hedge about a hundred yards from where he had been first shot at.

I never saw a quicker shot made, and Thornton himself was bound to admit that it was rather a "fluke."

CHAPTER VII.

" Figure-of-Four Traps," and how baited—Steel Trap on Wall—Long "Dead-
Falls "—Neighbouring Battue—Indian Corn—Pheasant Stacks—Wood-
Pigeons giving an Alarm—Other Sorts of Grain for Pheasants—Posts and
Rails to protect against "Long-netting "—Partridges and their "Jugging"
Places—"Bushing" the Ground—Proper Materials for the Purpose—
Different Kinds of Partridge Nets.

HAVING re-loaded, we waited for the small birds to alight again,
when Thornton let fly among them, and killed five.

These he wanted for baits for the stone traps. I had seen very
similar traps set in our garden when a boy, and naturally supposed
Thornton's to be the same in every particular. The original ones
had the principal notch cut in the "stretcher," and the bait was
frequently nibbled off by the mice, but the slate had not fallen.
Now, in Thornton's trap the centre support was an inch wide, and
the notch was cut in *that*, and only a shallow one in the "stretcher."
The consequence was that it fell at once. This made all the
difference between a bad trap and a first-rate one.

On arriving at one of them, Thornton tied a bird to the end of the
"stretcher," and gave it a cut with his knife. This was to cause
more scent either with birds or mice. He now proposed to go and
look at another steel trap at the farthest end of the wood. We made
a short cut through the bushes, and presently arrived at the rising of
a strong spring of water; which, following in its course, brought us
to the wall of the wood again. An exclamation from Thornton of
"Ha, ha!" was followed by the rattling of a chain, and, looking
towards the spot whence the sound proceeded, I saw an enormous cat
fast in a trap. It seems that the keeper had displaced a stone coping,
and set a trap in the space left; this trap had a cord tied to the
chain and fastened to a great stone lying on the ground. The chain
and cord together were just long enough (and no more) to reach the

trap. The cat had been walking along the wall, and set her foot in one of the round hawk traps placed there on purpose for poachers of her species. No bait was used, and Thornton said there was not a more fatal set for a cat than this, and the chain and cord were made the length I saw, so that the trap on being sprung must fall into the wood and not into the field. Were it otherwise it might be observed by a person casually passing by.

The keeper asked permission to have some long "trough" dead-falls made after a plan of his own. I told him to do just as he liked, and to show me one when made. These traps, it seems, were to set by wall or bank sides for small running vermin, and would require no bait. I gave Thornton leave to appropriate one of the rooms over my stable to the purposes of a workshop, and engaged to get a joiner's bench and a few tools so that he might do straightforward easy carpentering for himself. I had noticed that he seemed handy at it when putting bars to the gates.

While we were talking we heard a shot a good way off, and then another, and in fact a succession of them. It at once occurred to us both that a battue was being held by some one of my neighbours. It was early in the season for it (the end of the first week in October), but I was very glad to find they were commencing, as it would send us a pheasant or two, and perhaps some hares.

We sat down on a fallen tree to listen, and in about a quarter of an hour the quick eye of my companion detected a pheasant fly into the wood a very long way off. After the lapse of a quarter of an hour more three others came in all at once, and then two old cocks dropped within twenty yards of us. There was now a cessation of the sound of guns for a while, and then eight more shots in rapid succession. Thornton raised his hand very slowly and pointed along the wall-side. I looked and saw a hare sitting up and listen-ing. She cantered slowly down and came within two yards, and sat half looking at us and half behind her. We did not stir a hair's breadth, and in fact my eyes ran most painfully with not daring even to wink. In about two minutes she jogged into the wood, to our great delight.

We remained where we were for an hour, and had the satisfaction of seeing three more pheasants and five hares come in. Thornton expressed a hope that they would all stop, but knew it was more than we could well expect, as the pheasants would in a day or two run back again. As we had not dreamt about pheasant shooting beginning so early, no food had been put down for any stray arrivals. Thornton blamed himself for not having done it, but really we could not have anticipated the event. He was most impatient to get home and take the spring cart to buy some Indian corn, which food he had found by experience, he said, to be that most liked by pheasants. I told him to go as soon as possible; and he made such good use of his time, that he was back from the village by half-past two, and had fed the most likely spots in the wood. He found in his walks where three separate "pheasant stacks" had been made, and put the best part of the corn there.

One advantage my estate possessed in not having been preserved of late years was in the fact of there being but few wood-pigeons. These birds eat a terrible quantity of the pheasant's corn; and yet at the same time they do a certain amount of good in giving notice of trespassers in the woods, and especially in the breeding season, when pheasants' eggs are hunted for by poachers; not that pheasants lay chiefly in the woods, their constant favourite nesting-places being in clover or other green crops near a covert. As surely as any person walks through the woods, do the pigeons at once take alarm and fly rapidly to and fro at a great height above the trees, and by so doing must attract attention.

Indian corn possesses the advantage of being too large for the small birds to do much with. They will pick it up, certainly; and I have observed the large blue titmice holding it in their claws and hammering at the same grain for half an hour. Buckwheat, barley, peas, tick-beans, and raisins are favourites of the pheasant, but they will pass all these by for Indian corn. This at least was the opinion of Thornton, and he seemed to know something about it. He said that the practice was by no means uncommon for owners of plantations adjoining preserved lands to scatter such things as pheasants were fond of, and thus to draw their neighbour's game, and, without being at a farthing's-worth of expense in watching or trapping, to shoot the game thus attracted. He said that this had been done by a small landowner near the estate on which he (Thornton) had been keeper before coming to me, and he would have "gone a score miles to see him hung." Legitimate feeding, of course, was a different affair altogether; but when practised by a "killer," it could not be too strongly condemned. I quite entered into his feelings.

Very fortunately, he found that the pheasant stacks alluded to had been evidently made by a former keeper, who knew what he was about, and consequently would not require any repairs. It would have been awkward had the contrary been the case, as the hammering of nails, and driving of stakes, &c., would probably cause alarm in our newly-arrived game, nothing being so easily disturbed by noise as a pheasant.

Before returning home we went as far as the Moor-lane Quarry, and found it all quiet, the proprietors of the tent having taken their departure. I told Thornton I would have no more people allowed on the ground, as our rabbits would be taken to a certainty. We found a slight rabbit-scratching or two near the strongest holts, and this showed that they had taken to the place. The keeper had not yet seen any of our hares, and, in fact, had not much expectation of so doing for some days to come. As the rabbits, however, seemed reconciled to the locality, and there were a good lot turned down, we judged it advisable to protect the land adjoining in case a long net should be essayed. The quarry was situated in a plantation of young larch; the trees were about ten feet high, and just suited our purpose. We began therefore the next day by cutting down two or three score of them, and driving short posts into the ground, at intervals of about ten yards, along the plantation side. Each post stood at the end of a row, continued into the field about twenty-five yards. A rail was nailed to each post at six inches from the surface of the ground, and another a foot above that, making, in fact, a post-and-rail fence about twenty-one inches high. It was

utterly out of the question to set a net across these rails nearer of
course to the plantation than twenty-five yards, and at such a distance
you would get right amongst the nearest rabbits out at feed, when
the alarm (by a sharp stamp of the hind leg on the ground) would
instantly be given to their distant companions, and the result of the
netting expedition, of course, end in "signal" failure.

It was a very long job, but a necessary one, and I really liked the
occupation.

Oakes came to us while we were employed, and told me that the
covey of birds of which we had been told had run out of a stubble
field into a fallow only half an hour before, and had not suffered any
diminution in numbers since previously seen.   He considered, however, that the land where they belonged ought to be "bushed," and
that it would be soon done, as there were "only three grass fields
close about there."   He looked surprised when Thornton told him
that partridges would "jug" in stubbles or thin crops of turnips,
although certainly not so generally as grass lands.

The men agreed to have a turn at bushing next day, and to cut
the bushes in the nut wood, where we had started the men a few
days before, as there were among them some old stunted black-
thorns, just suited to the purpose.   The operation being, like most
others in the same line, a novelty to me, I went to see how it was
done.   Thornton said that in some parts of the country they guarded
the land against netting with hazel sticks thrust into the ground at
different angles, but the disadvantage of these was their invisibility
from a distance, a keeper having to walk to every field.   Another
plan was to cut small Scotch fir branches and trim the side twigs off,
and then to run the top part of the stem into the ground.   These
made good defences, but they also were rather invisible, and,
besides, cattle might possibly lie down on them in the dark and
get injured.

The thorn bushes could be seen from a good distance, and, being
stuck in the ground only fast enough to prevent being blown away
by the wind, would, if caught by a net, instantly draw out and roll
up in it, and this once done, they were awkward affairs to set free

again, and time would be lost, and the nets probably be damaged ; the clearing a net by night being a very different matter from doing so by day. It must be admitted, however, that a partridge net is wonderfully strong, being made of the best silk, so as not to take up room, to be easily "worked," and not to absorb wet.

The bushing is, of course, to prevent the use of the "sheet" or "clap" partridge net. There is another sort, called a "tunnel" net, and this is used where the land is laid down in "ridge and furrow." The net being set in a furrow, the birds may be gently driven into it by the aid of a horse, and, if there are no furrows, the same end is accomplished at a gate. The sheet net is, however, used in ninety-nine cases out of a hundred.

CHAPTER VIII.

Pheasant Stacks; how constructed—Marking Rides in Covert—Trespasser
detected—Randall and Scourfield appearing before the Magistrates—The
Dress and Appearance of my Keepers—Ruse on the Part of Thornton—
Evidence before Magistrates—Description of Poacher's Gun—A stupid
Witness in another Case.

THE next day, by appointment with Thornton, I went to the large
wood to see whether any of our pheasant corn was gone, and we
were very glad to find that a good deal had been taken, and by
pheasants, too.   I had now an opportunity of seeing how the stacks
were made.   Four posts had been driven into the ground, inclosing
a square of about six feet.   Rails were nailed to each post, and
cross-pieces laid across these, allowing intervals of about six inches.
The corn being stacked on this framing was then thatched, and tied
on with tarred cord ; of course the straw was all decayed away from
those we found, but the framing was still good, having been made of
old larch sawn up, which will last as long as oak.   I should mention
that the height of the frame from the ground was about eighteen inches.

I gave Thornton orders to get what oat straw he wanted, and let
the stacks be built up again and thatched.

Having seen to all this, we took a short cut to our nearest trap,
and on the way thither we crossed one of the grass rides of the
covert.   Thornton asked me to wait a minute, while he went a short
distance along it.   He soon returned, with the intimation that some
one had been down this ride since the evening before, as he had
marked it by stretching a black thread across.   I went back to look
at his mode of marking, and found the thread tied to a tree on one
side of the ride and hung loosely over a bough on the other, about
three feet from the ground.   It was, of course, at once evident that
we had had a trespasser through the wood, and very probably one
of the tenants' labourers.   Thornton said he had taken a look round

the evening before, and had sent Oakes in a totally different direction. When he visited the wood himself, the thread was not disturbed, and the night had been very still. Whoever had knocked it down had been totally unconscious of having done so.

With newly-arrived pheasants it would never do to have the coverts invaded by people passing through them night and morning, so the keeper agreed to watch that evening for the chance of the person coming again.

In due course he made his report that the aggressor had appeared at about half-past six, and that he was a day labourer employed at the tan-works, about a couple of miles off. He was after no mischief, but merely took that road as a short cut to his home. Having been warned not to trespass again, he gave the required promise to desist, and there was an end of it. Had the ride not been marked, this trespass (although, after all, not a serious one) would probably have been continued for some time, and intelligence of our game communicated to those who ought not to know about it.

After the lapse of about a week the time arrived when Messrs. Randall and Scourfield had to appear before the magistrates in accordance with the summonses issued against them.

Thornton had not gone for "trespass," but for "shooting without a certificate." He said he had generally found such a leaning towards a poacher, and such a disposition to treat *him* as an ill-used individual, and *not the landowner*, whose game he had taken, that he always ignored the case of simple game-trespass where he could, and went for the penalty for the offence above alluded to. In several instances he had found the magistrates letting some hardened poaching rascal off by payment of some five or ten shillings fine and costs, on the assumption that the informer would proceed for the other penalty, which in nine cases out of ten was never done.

On the morning of the petty sessions we set off in my spring cart —viz., myself, Thornton, and Oakes. I was very proud of the appearance of my two companions, I must say. Thornton was dressed in a new brown velveteen shooting-jacket and waistcoat (each as full of pockets as it would hold), drab breeches, long gaiters, and lace-up boots—these latter polished to a miracle. He had on a low-crowned black hat, and was so beautifully shaven that one would almost have thought another hair would never grow on his chin. Being a very good-looking, dark-whiskered fellow, I looked at him with very great admiration, and made a favourable mental comparison between this fine English keeper and a French *garde-chasse* with his uniform and cocked hat !

Oakes by no means disgraced us by his appearance, being got up in a style somewhat similar to that of his superior officer. *His* attending us was part of a plan of the great Mr. Thornton, into which I was initiated. He observed that it would spread fast enough that we were all gone to the petty sessions, and if Oakes were seen to accompany us it would be considered a fine opportunity for a day's ferreting by anyone having an inclination that way. Oakes had been "put up" to this, and he had let drop casually amongst one or two people the fact of his being likely to accompany us on the eventful day. We had two towns within driving distance at which petty sessions were held on alternate Saturdays, and the one to which we had to go was about eight miles off, instead of only four, as would have been the case had the summonses been deferred.

Our departure was observed by several casual passengers on the road, and when we had proceeded about a mile from home, and the hedges permitted of no extended view, Oakes got down and betook himself, under cover of the walls and fences, to a spot from whence he could pretty well command a view of the approaches to our small larch wood where the rabbits were. Here we will leave him, and proceed with our main history.

On arriving at the principal inn we had the horse put up, and then walked down to the town hall. Two or three gentlemanly-looking men were standing at the door talking, and one of them came up to me and, accosting me by name, begged to make himself known as Mr. Reynardson, the senior magistrate in that neighbourhood. He alluded to my arrival amongst them, and begged to know if I were prepared to receive visitors, as he and his neighbouring friends were anxious to make my acquaintance. I, of course, met these advances

E

in the cordial spirit with which they were made. Mr. Reynardson
then introduced me amongst his friends, and requested I would sit
with them on the bench, hoping, as they kindly expressed it, that I
should before long do so as a brother magistrate, and not merely as
an amateur. I duly made my acknowledgments, and accepted the
civility, stating, however, that I would defer so doing until after my
keeper's case had been heard.

Mr. Reynardson told me that mine was not the only case of the
kind that morning. It seems that another man had been caught
shooting grouse on Sir Astley Wallington's moor: "And I hope,"
said my companion, "that your man will give his evidence better
than Sir Astley's; for we've had him before, and although he means
well enough, and does not wish to state more than he knows, yet,
what with his refusing to answer some questions, fencing with
others, and his general stupidity, we have often found it difficult to
convict. Now from what I see of your keeper—I suppose that is the
man, that good-looking fellow in the brown velveteen—I imagine he
is a different sort of a witness; he appears an intelligent, sharp
fellow." I told Mr. Reynardson I had never had the opportunity of
seeing Thornton as a witness, and could not, of course, speak to it.

The time for opening the court had now arrived, and my case was
the first called on. Messrs. Scourfield and Randall duly appeared,
and they were assisted by eminent counsel in the person of a Mr.
Sharpham, who was a little "hard-bitten" man, with a very comical-
looking face, and stiff brushed-up black hair.

Thornton gave his evidence slowly, and in as few words as he
could, so as to allow the magistrates' clerk to take it all down
without difficulty. Having stated all he knew, he was asked by Mr.
Sharpham whether he "knew that he was on his oath." Thornton
admitted that amount of knowledge at once. He was then asked
how he could see a man shoot when he himself was lying on the
other side the wall. He replied that "he did not see him shoot."
"Then how do you know that either of these men killed that
grouse?" "Because, sir," Thornton replied, "a shot went close to
where I was; one man jumped over the wall to pick up a grouse I

saw knocked off it, and the other also came over and helped him, and they 'gathered' the bird." He was then asked how far he was from the men when they jumped over; and he replied, "about twenty yards." A great amount of cross-questioning now commenced as to whether it might not be thirty yards, or fifty, but Thornton merely kept to the answer, "about twenty yards." The next question was: "You say you went with them to where the two guns stood. How do you know that those were their guns?" "I knew Scourfield's gun at once," was the reply. "How could you know it?" And here Mr. Thornton entered into a minute description of the gun that amused the magistrates and the court extremely. It was as follows: It had only one ramrod pipe, which was dented all round, and opened in front by rough usage till it was like the bell of a cornopean; the sight was knocked off, and the ramrod was sticking out about six inches, evidently from the kicking of the gun; the hammer was down, and the cap blackened and spread out.

There was no standing against all this evidence, and both men were convicted in the half penalty and costs. Application was made for time to pay, but this was at once refused; and although they declared they had not a farthing to pay with, and would go to gaol, yet the money was forthcoming before half an hour had elapsed; and, judging from the sum produced by Randall, the *full* penalty would have been as easily met. I now took a seat amongst the magistrates, and William Heath, under-keeper to Sir Astley Wallington, stepped into the box.

He stated that he was out watching early in the morning, and was concealed in a hole amongst the heath. He saw a man (the defendant) get over the wall and beat the moor. Another man was standing in the road ready to give the alarm. A grouse got up. and the man on the moor shot at it, and, after a short chase, secured it. The keeper ran this man and got within a dozen yards of him, but, finding he was too quick on the legs, called out, "Well, I know you, Moth; so you may run if you like!" The other man had bolted, and Heath, although morally certain of his identity, would

E 2

not swear to him. Now, here was a clear enough case, yet Heath did all he could to damage his own evidence. He was asked how near he was to Moth when he shot, and he said, "About eighty yards." Mr. Sharpham: "Would it be 150 yards?" Heath: "Well, it might be." Mr. S.: "Was it 200 yards?" Heath: "No, hardly." Mr. S.: "You won't swear it was not 250 yards?" Heath: "It might be, but I don't know." Mr. S.: "Then you won't swear it wasn't?" Heath: "No." Mr. S.: "Have you ever told anyone that you shouldn't like to say it was Moth for certain?" Heath: "Have I told anyone I shouldn't like to say it was Moth for certain?" Mr. S.: "Yes, yes. There's not the least necessity to be repeating all my words." (Heath silent.) Mr. S.: "Come, sir, answer me." Heath: "What should I tell anyone for?" Mr. S.: "Nay, you must not ask *me*. Answer my question." Heath: "I don't know as I ever did." Mr. S.: "Oh, then, you won't swear you haven't?" Heath: "Won't swear I haven't?" Mr. S.: "Yes, won't swear you haven't." Heath: "Not as I know on."

In the face of this, what could be done? The keeper had *not* told anyone, simply because he never had any doubt about the identity of the man, and yet those who did not know Heath would at once set him down as an untrustworthy witness. One of the magistrates, by a few judicious questions, showed, at last, that Heath was afraid of being pulled to pieces by the lawyer, and this made him so stupid and apparently unreliable.

After it was over, Mr. Reynardson complimented Thornton on the way in which he gave his evidence, and added that it was always the same with Heath, and although he had secured several convictions, yet he had failed in others, to the great indignation of his master, who disliked taking a "bad case" into court; and, in fact, it was a toss-up whether a first-rate one would not break down when resting on the evidence of this man. He went on to say that, a few months before, Heath had found two men with "snap" dogs, beating one of the small plantations. He was asked what they were beating for, and, instead of saying at once "for hares," said "I don't know." He was asked, "Have you any hares in that plantation?" To

which he replied, " Yes, there's hares."   " And rabbits ?"   "I dare
say."   The next question was, "Are there any squirrels ?"   To
which he replied, "I think so."   "Oh, then, you won't swear these
men were not after them ?"   Answer, "No."   "Now," asked my
informant, " how could one convict those fellows ?"   It was clearly
impossible.

CHAPTER IX.

Oakes catches some Poachers—Ferreting Rabbits—Long " Dead-Fall ; " how made—Snow, Hares not moving in—Freeholder shooting the Hares—Sheep in Snow-Drift.

OUR expedition had detained us till four o'clock, and soon after that hour we had the horse put in again and drove home. The gate going into my stable-yard was opened by Oakes, who bore a respectful grin on his countenance, which at once spoke volumes, and in fact he could hardly contain himself during our descent from the spring-cart. " Well, Oakes," I said, " so you've got them ?" " Yes, sir, I've got 'em safe enough," was the reply. I directed him to come into the house and let me know all about it. It seems that he had not been planted more than half an hour when he observed a man come out of the footpath and go into the Scourfields' yard, from which he emerged in a few minutes with old Scourfield. They sat on the wall together, and kept occasionally shading their eyes in the direction of the road coming from the station, which road led also past the tan-works. Before long a man was seen coming along this road, and he was apparently the expected arrival, for as soon as he got up to the cottage the man on the wall jumped down, and they both started in the direction of the quarry. Oakes had his glass out, and at once saw that one of these men was George Woodhall, and the other was Richard Brett, both well known to him. Woodhall had often boasted that no one could ever find him " at work " (that is. poaching), and, even if such a thing were to happen, he " would never be taken." I shall continue the story in the first person, and let Oakes tell it in his own words.

" Knowing that Woodhall kept a ferret, I guessed at once they would make for the quarry, and a very difficult job I found it to get there before them, as they could, as you know, sir, see every

inch of the road almost between where I was clapped at Stenson's
shed and the Quarry Wood. When they got to that dip in the lane,
I set off and ran as hard as ever I could, and managed to get the
brow between me and them before they saw me. It was easy enough
then, and I bolted into the planting, but did not know hardly where
to hide when I got there. At last I thought of the old smithy, and
I run down to it, and waited to see if I could make 'em out from
there. I hadn't been more than a few minutes when I sees 'em
both coming, and 'By George,' says I, 'they're coming in!' Luckily,
there was a dark spot behind the cooling-trough, so I clapped down,
and just as I did so they entered. Brett says, 'We'll try thine first,
and keep mine to be fresh, for them there's strongish spots for a odd
ferret to work.' Woodhall says, 'Ah! let's turn him into the old
trough and clap summat over him; he'll be fresher running about
than kept in the bag.' They rooted about, and couldn't find anything to put over the trough, so I heard them pulling the boards out
of the roof; and at last they made the ferret safe, and left the smithy.
They were within a yard of me all the while, but luckily it's very
dark in that corner, and I was clapped well down. I then got up
and followed 'em by guess, but found I was right. I went first
towards where the biggest ridding had been done, for it used to be a
noted place for rabbits when there was some a few years ago. Sure
enough there they were, and I let 'em set four purse nets at some
odd holes, and two rattling great sheet nets as took in all the shaks"
—I suppose Mr. Oakes meant "shakes" in the rock—"where the
stone had been followed. They was regular good hands at ferreting,
and no mistake. They didn't speak a word, but did it all as quiet
as mice, and they stepped about as silent as if they had no boots on.
There wasn't any wind, so it didn't matter which road they set. By
crawling flat on my chest I got close above 'em, when the nets was
all down, and then Woodhall made a bit of a sign with his hand,
and Brett gave him the ferret out of his bag, and Woodhall chucked
him quietly into the topmost hole. In about a minute I heard a
'thungeing,' and they heard it too, and gave a look at each other.
At one time it came right under where I was, and then it was all

quiet; at last it begun again, and out came a rabbit. I jumped
up and shouted, ' That'll do, George, you needn't kill him !'   They
just gave one look, and bolted off as hard as ever they could go.
Brett made a grab at one of the sheet nets, but missed of it.   I
wanted the other ferret as well, so I run the men as hard as I
could to get them away, for if I had not they might have bolted
into the old smithy, and got the ferret as they'd left, and I knew I
was safe of the one in the hole.   It was just as I thought ; they
were meaning to have him, but I was so close a-top of 'em that
they went on, and no doubt they thought they could come and fetch
the ferret when it was all safe.   I went back and found two more
rabbits in the purse nets, and one of the gate nets rolled a dozen
yards away.   I put the three rabbits in my pocket, and collected
the nets, and then I had about an hour's waiting ; but at last the
ferret came out, and I catched him.   He were not coped or anything.
I then went and got the other, and of course as soon as I could I
turned the rabbits in again.   As I hadn't a ferret-bag, it was a
very awkward matter bringing the two ferrets home, but luckily
they were two very quiet 'uns, and I've got 'em in the old corn bin.
They're a good lot of nets, too, sir.

   Altogether Oakes seemed to have shown very good generalship,
and he duly received the applause of myself and Thornton.   It was
fortunate, too, that none of the rabbits had been worried.   The
ferret must, of course, in each instance have gone back again after
bolting them, instead of following them up in the purse nets.   The
only way in which it could be accounted for was by the fact of
the strings being extra long, as is usually the case with the purse net
used by poachers, which allows of the pegs catching between two of
the coping stones of a wall, instead of requiring them to be thrust
into the ground.   The ferret, therefore, in this instance, not seeing
the rabbit struggling close by, and not perhaps caring to follow the
scent, had, very fortunately, gone back into the rock in search of a
fresh rabbit.

   Thornton's work-bench and joiner's tools being ready for him, he
occupied himself on the Monday morning in making one of the long

dead-fall traps, which he finished by noon. It was about three feet long by eleven inches deep inside, and three inches wide. A treadle worked in the bottom of the box on two brass pins. One of these came through the side, and had on it a sort of finger about a couple of inches long, terminating in a sharp point. There was a spring fastened to the side of the box, with its end (also pointed) just wrapping over the finger alluded to. A couple of strong screws were fastened into the side of the trap, with a notch in the head of each, into which a short piece of iron would catch. The weight to crush the vermin was a piece of three-inch square deal, about an inch shorter than the whole trap. Across the top of the opening, and just in the centre, was a piece of hard wood, with a hole bored and burnt through. The heavy weight was attached by an old boot-lace to the small cross-piece of iron. To set the trap you had to press the spring down and turn the treadle till the finger caught on the end of the spring. The cross-bit was placed in the notch, and the weight then kept suspended in the trap, evenly balanced. Any small vermin running through, and passing over the treadle, caused it to tilt on one side, and the spring being released, it flew out and knocked the cross-piece of iron away, and the weight, of course, falling, crushed the weasel or stoat, and killed it instantaneously. The trap seemed wonderfully quick in its action, going off almost like a gun, it was so rapid. The treadle, I should have said, was a foot long, and the whole trap being three feet, the vermin could not possibly escape, as, from whichever way it entered, that particular end of the treadle must be pressed, and there was then, of course, two feet of trap to allow for. Thornton said he always rubbed the spring and finger with mercurial (or what is commonly called blue) ointment, and the weather had no effect upon them.

We took this trap down to the wood, and set it in a dry ditch under one of the hedges leading to the wood, and piled up a few stones, so that any small vermin running up the ditch must necessarily pass through the trap. It remained without being let off for three days. On the fourth Thornton found a rat in it, and on looking at it the day after he found a weasel caught in the morning, and another the same evening. These were both of them "Jill" or female weasels, and, not weighing much more than good well-conditioned field-mice, spoke most favourably of the capabilities of the trap.

There are other traps of apparently the same kind; but in the trap we used the treadle was independent of the weight, while in the common ones the weight is always straining on the treadle, and so renders them liable to remain unsprung if any light vermin passes through.

Nothing in our daily routine of preserving happened for a considerable time. Woodhall and Brett were duly summoned, and duly fined. They made a great demand for their ferrets, but the application was contemptuously ignored. No claim of the kind could be legally entertained, and very indignant they were in consequence.

Two or three of our hares had been seen near the Black Inclosure, and two or three in the grass rides of the large wood, and the pheasants had stopped with us pretty well. Thornton had gone very frequently on still evenings to "roost them up," and had heard on an average about five go up.

We had now arrived at December, and about the middle of that month a pretty heavy fall of snow came. This was an anxious time for my two keepers, as "tracing" would probably be commenced, it being known that Messrs. Scourfield and Randall were not the only "gun men" in the district. Thornton and Oakes had an understanding with the neighbouring keepers that they should assist each other in following poachers on to their respective territories. The first day of the snow, but few tracings of hares were to be seen—and, in fact, I ascertained this by personal observation in a long round I took. I mentioned this fact to Thornton with some chagrin, but he told me not to annoy myself about this, as hares very seldom shift about after or during the first night of a snow. I had no reason to find fault with the apparent deficiency of rabbits, as the ground near their locality was famously trampled with them. I found that Thornton was right in what he advanced, for the day after I went

the same round, and was very much satisfied with the number of
hare "feetings," as Thornton called them.

Our boundaries being rather extensive, we arranged to take
separate beats, so as to leave no part of the estate unprotected.
We had the greatest reason to fear losing hares on the "outside,"
and especially about that part of my land joining up to the small
freeholder, who, we were afraid, would not only look with indiffer-
ence on any poaching excursions over his estate, but probably
transact a little tracing business on his own account. As we feared,
so it turned out. We did not suffer from the depredations of anyone
ourselves during this storm, but on the property alluded to my
neighbour was very busy, and shot two hares under the very nose of
Mr. Thornton himself. Poor Thornton told me of it, and almost
cried with indignation; but what could one do? I was very glad to
hear that Thornton had made no remark, although the affair
happened within fifty yards of him.

The snow commenced again the same night, and before morning
was of very great depth. Thornton and Oakes were going their
rounds at daybreak, and betook themselves in the direction of this
very land, hoping to turn any hares from it. The snow was very
deep, and had drifted half-way up the hedges.

On arriving within sight of this freeholder's estate, what was
their surprise to see his wife making her way through the snow as
well as she could, with a hayfork in her hand! Without asking her
permission they both went up to her, and begged to know what she
could be dreaming of in coming out on such a morning. It seems
that her husband (whose name, if I have not previously mentioned
it, was Serley) had caught a bad attack of rheumatism while
tracing the day before, and was confined to his bed. The knowledge
that all his sheep were out in the snow had much disconcerted him;
and, what was worse, his wife could not get anyone to assist in
finding them, and was compelled to go herself. I am afraid that
our friend's well-known character for stinginess and general disagree-
ableness did not tend towards encouraging the advances of his
neighbours.

Thornton and Oakes, as I said, at once went and offered their help, for which she, in her way, tendered her thanks. They insisted that she should go back, as it was not fit for a woman to be out in such a storm, and begged her to assure Mr. Serley that his sheep should be found if it were possible, and Oakes accompanied her home for the purpose of procuring another fork.

An hour's probing in the snowdrifts disclosed the whereabouts of one sheep, and, continuing their search, they gradually arrived at the whole flock, consisting of eighteen.

CHAPTER X.

Thornton and Oakes make Friends with Mr. Serley—Arden's Anecdote of Poachers in the Snow—Poisoning Carrion-Crows and Magpies—We watch them take the Poison—Rooks taking Eggs—Plovers discriminating between Rooks and Crows—Feeding Hares and Rabbits and Grouse—Hares frequenting public Roads.

HAVING rescued the sheep, which were not very much the worse for their temporary concealment, the two keepers took them down to Serley's strawyard, and were requested by his wife to come in and see the master. Being shown up into his bedroom, they found him sitting before a good fire, and rather easier. He expressed numberless obligations to Thornton and Oakes for their ready assistance, and the former had the good taste to observe that their master (meaning myself) would be as glad as Mr. Serley was to find his men had had it in their power to help him as they had done. Serley remarked that on the only occasion on which I had seen him the question of assistance to his sheep had been brought up; "and you may tell Mr. Houston," said he, "that he may go over my land whenever he likes, and so may you, Mr. Thornton, and George here, too. I shot a brace of hares yesterday, and I saw one of you watching, and I daresay you were fine and vexed; but, unless I am regular short of a hare, depend upon it I shall let 'em alone in future." Thornton assured him he need never want for a hare or a couple of rabbits when we had enough to give away, but that at present we were doing all we could to get them up.

Mr. Serley offered them some breakfast, but they declined taking any, and parted with mutual expressions of goodwill.

I was very glad indeed to find things had turned out so agreeably, as *that* freehold was always a sort of "thorn in my side."

The same afternoon a change of the wind set in, and the snow rapidly disappeared. A day or two afterwards I happened to be going from home, and as I was walking to the station I met Arden, and, having plenty of time, I stopped to have a chat and a comparison of "keepering" notes with him. He told me of a very clever catch he had made during the snow ; and although it is not every locality that will allow of its being carried out, yet such is possible.

In one of their plantations, consisting chiefly of larch, with a few large and bushy spruce, are some strong rabbit burrows. Arden had had these burrows ferreted by poachers more than once ; and the plantation being situated on a hill, it was easy for one poacher to look out while the other was occupied with ferreting. Snow being on the ground rendered the approach of a keeper almost an impossibility without being seen.

Arden had been turning the matter over in his mind, and at last hit upon the following plan. He started off before daylight, and passed through the plantation within about four feet of a very thickly-feathered spruce, and close also to some much-used burrows. He made a very considerable round, and came back again *exactly on his own footsteps.* When at the spruce I have mentioned, he reached over to it, and managed to swing himself with one foot on to a lower bough. This once achieved, the rest was easy enough. Very fortunately, there had been a good deal of wind, and the snow consequently had not lain on the branches. About half-past eight o'clock he was startled by the arrival of two men, who passed close under the tree, having evidently been hunting Arden's back track.

They were by no means confident, however, and spoke to each other in a low tone of voice, and stopped about a dozen yards off. One of them then went to the fence of the plantation, and Arden heard him say, "All right—he's come in here." The other one then joined him, and they were evidently looking carefully all round in the distance.

At last they seemed assured that all must be right, and leaving one to keep watch, the other came straight back to the burrows, close to Arden's place of concealment. The man now produced a bag from his pocket, out of which he took a ferret, and, looking at it

carefully to make sure the "coping" was not come undone, he
turned it into the burrow, and in a few seconds had four purse-nets
set. His companion now gave a low whistle, and on the instant the
man stooped, in the attitude of seizing the nearest net. Another
whistle seemed to be a signal that all was right again. Arden could
now hear the rabbits banging about under ground, but it was many
minutes before one would bolt. At last one did so, and was killed
in an instant. Arden kept perfectly quiet, and it was now evident
that the ferret had got a rabbit fast in a corner, and that it would
not come out.

The man called very softly, "Jem!" and received the answer,
"Now!"

"Come here, lad, she's fast," was the reply; "I can hear her
thirking like ought."

Jem came up, and knelt down to listen for a good while, during
which period his companion went back to see if all was safe. As it
apparently was so, he returned to the burrow, and also lay down to
listen. All of a sudden they both flew to their feet, with the
subdued exclamation, "Her's here!" and out came a rabbit. It was
seized instantly—and just then the voice of Mr. Arden was heard to
remark from overhead, "It's a nice 'un, Tommy!" The men looked
up perfectly horrified, and Arden deliberately came down the tree.

The one named "Tommy" begged Arden not to take any steps
in the matter, and they were temporarily reassured by being told
that "he'd say no more about it *if his master was agreeable*, but that
he must *just ask him first*."

The snow had not disappeared more than a week, when the wind
changed round again, and another heavy fall came, and hard frost
with it. I named previously that we had a few carrion-crows about,
and there were also the magpies remaining out of the large lot that
roosted in the larch plantation, and whose numbers we had so much
reduced during our evening's amusement in the autumn. Thornton
had not devoted much time towards them, as he meant to try what
he could do with poison in the hard weather.

As the snow lay on the ground without any perceptible diminution,

owing to the frost, Thornton appeared one morning with four dead
rats that had been given him by one of the farmers, and expressed
his intention of setting them for the carrion-crows and magpies.
He procured some suet from my cook, and having melted this with
a small quantity of butter, he made it up into pills about the size
of a boy's marble. I had given him some strychnine, which he
carried in a very small bottle, with a bit of wire run through the
cork and flattened out at the end. Having made an incision down
each rat, so as to show plenty of red, he next made a hole in each
of the bits of suet and inserted about a quarter of a grain of
strychnine.

We started off for that part of the estate where the crows and
magpies were mostly to be seen, and close under a very large Scotch
fir, near the Black Inclosure, he pegged one of the rats down to
the ground. By using considerable exertion he managed to get up
the tree, and on one of the lower boughs plastered a bit of the suet,
taking care, however, not to spread it out more than necessary.
The poison was thus placed beyond the reach of a dog or fox.

We then proceeded to a part of the plantation where an old shed
stood, and placed another rat, and on the walls of the building (the
roof being gone) Thornton put two more bits of suet, about four
yards from each other. We now had to go about half a mile, as a
wall was required for another set, and having arrived at one, he
pegged down both the other rats, and put suet at intervals of about
four yards, in five different places, on the top of this wall. Nothing
interfered with any of our baits till the day but one after, and on
that day I went round with my keeper, and at the spot where we
had put the greatest number of pieces we found all gone, and four
magpies lying dead. The rat was very much pecked, and Thornton,
who had previously prepared some more of the suet-pills, renewed
the baits on the wall. He told me the reason for putting them
some distance apart was to guard as much as possible against one
carrion-crow or magpie taking all the pieces; and, as it was, one had
taken two of the pills, as instanced by five baits being gone and
only four magpies killed. While he was putting the suet on to the

coping, I saw a pair of carrion-crows a great distance off, but making
their way in the direction of the Scotch fir to which I have alluded.
They did not appear at first disposed to settle on the tree, but were
flying about a hundred yards past it. Suddenly they both turned
and settled on the identical tree. We both had our glasses out
instantly to watch their movements. One of the carrion-crows,
after the lapse of a quarter of an hour, flew down and settled in the
field about fifty yards from the rat, and having walked towards it
for a short distance, rose up and settled on the tree again. After
remaining at least another quarter of an hour they both flew down,
and this time within a few feet of the rat. They were evidently
rather suspicious even yet, and one of them went into the tree,
and to our great delight, and amid our breathless expectation,
swallowed the bit of suet. In less than a dozen seconds he seemed
to be taken giddy, and after a heave or two backwards and forwards
turned back-downwards under the bough, flapping his wings violently,
and then dropped to the ground. The other crow, seeing evidently
that something was "up," took a flight round once or twice, and
then settled close to the poisoned one, and began pecking him on
the head as hard as he could.

Having tried this course of surgical treatment for some time, and
finding it attended with no beneficial result, he took himself off,
and, as he went in the direction of our other bait, we did not attempt
to follow him then. In the afternoon, however, we determined to go
and see if he had paid a visit to the old shed, and, sure enough, he
was there, and past all human aid too. One piece of suet only was
gone. I suppose he had not seen the other, but had at once flown
down after taking his preliminary dose, and he lay within a foot of
the rat. Thornton knew of other carrion-crows, so he re-baited the
shed wall, and before the week was over had poisoned six more
crows, and then the rooks found it out ; and this being a tolerable
sign that the carrion-crows were extirpated, and as it would never
do to have the poor rooks poisoned, we put no more strychnine.
During this week we got also seventeen more magpies.

After rooks have been pinched by a few days' frost and snow,

F

they will take poisoned meat just as readily as carrrion-crows do, and in the laying season will also take the eggs of partridges and pheasants; not that they hunt systematically for them, but if they find a nest in their travels they suck every egg, as a matter of course. Now crows and magpies are *always* on the look-out for such things, and, in fact, "make a business of it." During the time that green plovers are laying their eggs, if a rook passes their territory little or no notice is taken or remark made; but the instant a carrion-crow essays the same route, all the plovers in the neighbourhood are at him uttering their loudest cries, and "dusting" him with their wings.

The continued snow put my neighbour's good resolutions rather severely to the test, but he did not attempt the lives of any hares, and for this I had an opportunity before long of tendering my acknowledgments. In fact, we all became great friends, and Mr. Thornton came in for an invitation to supper at Mr. Serley's house during the Christmas week, and made himself so agreeable, I suppose, that the invitation was extended to a request that he would "drop in any time he went that way."

By Thornton's wishes I had a good quantity of mountain ash and thorn boughs cut off and spread about in the covers for the rabbits and hares, and he, in fact, took a walk of nearly three miles, for a large quantity of Irish ivy, which was growing on the wall of a pinfold. The snow was frozen so hard that even the rabbits found a difficulty in scratching through the coating of ice. I had also a score or two of sheaves of oats put on the moor for the grouse, and when the oats were getting nearly consumed, had them replaced with more.

To my great gratification I received from Oakes the announcement that he had one morning put up two grey hens, and no time was lost in making a stack of corn for them in the wood called the Black Inclosure, where they were seen. It is difficult to account for the preference grouse and black game show to oats over other sorts of corn. The only fact that explains it is, I suppose, that oats are the kind of grain more usually met with in localities frequented by them;

and yet exceptions do occur of wheat and barley being grown in their neighbourhood, but being neglected for oats where they also are obtainable.

I had no reason to be dissatisfied with the traces of hares, take it altogether, but they *would* frequent the public roads so invariably. Naming this to the keeper, I learnt that, after a hare has fed, she always betakes herself to the driest spots, for the purpose of getting rid of the wet that clings to the short stubby hair on her feet; and at daybreak a hare may be observed to canter along a road, and occasionally to stop and jerk each of her feet outwards with a sharp movement, and this is for the purpose of driving out the wet, which, in fact, may sometimes be seen to fly off in a few drops. She then betakes herself to her seat for the day.

CHAPTER XI.

Mr. Houston finds Hangs set in a casual Walk—Consultation with Thornton, and his Proposal for discovering the Poacher—Arrangement with Farm Tenant—Discrimination on the Part of Oakes—He catches the Setter of the Hangs.

I HAPPENED to take a walk, one very fine frosty morning, to some high open ground about a mile from home, for the purpose of seeing the view, which from the upper part of it was very extensive. The land itself was rented by a most respectable hard-working man, who farmed in the best possible style for our part of the country. His fields were patterns of neatness. Such a thing as a thistle was not to be observed in any one of them. The gates were all in good order, and the fences beautifully trimmed and small. The height of these latter was about three feet, and they were cut in a slanting direction from the ground up to an edge as thin as one's hand. From the nature of the soil and its lying so completely on a gradual slope, no ditches were needed, and you could see from one field into another for at least five hundred yards round.

I had lounged about for nearly an hour when I, by the merest chance, caught sight of a "support" to a "hang" in one of the hedges. I believe it was the white cut on the top of the little peg that first attracted my eye. Acting upon a sudden and perhaps fortunate impulse, I did not stoop down to investigate the whole apparatus, but continued my walk down the hedge-side, and became aware in so doing of the presence of eleven more of these snares. When I got home I found Oakes in the yard cleaning a curious old rifle that had got very rusty, and which I had that morning given to him to put into order.

On telling him of my discovery, he confessed he did not know who to "judge" in the matter, as he was not aware of any of the farm labourers being addicted to that sort of amusement. The tenant of the land (Jervase Hayes by name) was, Oakes assured me, the last person to allow or connive at such proceedings on the part of any of his men. At all events, one thing was certain, the hangs must be watched ; but now a great difficulty arose—where must they be watched from ? I suggested that Thornton and Oakes should be concealed where there was covert, which would be in the nearest thick hedge, and that they should from thence observe the movements of the person who should come to look at, or remove, any of the hangs. This plan, however, Oakes negatived, as the chances, and in fact probabilities, were that the poacher would come the first thing in the morning or the last at night, and then the distance at which the keepers would be concealed must militate against a successful capture of the depredator.

In an emergency like the present who could be so likely to hit upon a good plan as the great Mr. Thornton ? So I dispatched Oakes to bring him to the house. In an hour he arrived, and had been fully informed by Oakes of our difficulty on the way. His "mighty mind " rose superior to the occasion, which puzzled feeble mortals like my under-keeper and myself, and he was all ready with a proposition. The following was the *contour* of his arrangements.

I was to go in the morning and see my tenant Hayes, and tell him at once the state of the case, safely trusting to his not divulging it, or the plan by which I intended to circumvent the setter of the hangs. I was to propose to build him a shed on this open land, and previously to our actually commencing it, the fields were to be tried in several places, to see where stone lay most conveniently to the surface. I was myself to superintend the search, and two or three " trial holes " were to be made, but none of them suspiciously near the hedge. When made, it was of course the intention of either Thornton or Oakes, or both, to be duly hid in one or more of them.

The plan seemed an admirable one, but I could see that Oakes was most impatiently waiting for his superior to finish, evidently prepared with a fatal objection.

It was as I had expected, and the objection consisted of the following: "Well, but what about to-morrow morning?"   "Don't frighten yourself, George," was the reply.   "Get me a drop of benzine, and I'll make that all right.   I can't, of course, stop a hare being taken to night, perhaps; but we must run our chance of that."

Unfortunately, I had no benzine, but I had naphtha, and Thornton said he thought it would do as well. I gave him about half a gallon, and as soon as ten o'clock had struck, he and Oakes started off with a dark lantern, and, with its aid, they had no difficulty in finding the hangs, and, in fact, four more, making fifteen in all. The hangs had, it seems, been set by a regular "old hand." The strings were not tied to pegs stuck in the ground, but they were made fast to the lower strong shoots in the hedge, so that a hare, instead of having a dead pull by which she might snap the string, was subject to the action of a *strong spring*, which by her struggles would render her *hors de combat* in half the time.

The keepers found to their satisfaction that none of the hangs had, as yet, done anything.   Had any one of them caught, it would have been evident enough from the tearing of the ground, and the bits of "dawn" sprinkled about.

Ten minutes sufficed to render them all harmless for two or three days, by the operation of spilling a little of the naphtha within a yard of each hang on both sides of the hedge.   By way of encouraging the setter of them, they "ran" one of the hangs, by drawing up the noose and stretching it out at full length, to make it appear as if it had caught and missed.

The next morning my part of the performance had to be carried out, so I set off to Hayes' farm, and found him very busy with one of his labourers opening a drain in the stackyard.   He was about to leave his occupation to attend to me, but I told him to go on, as I could say what I wished to tell him without interfering with his work.

Poor Hayes pricked up his ears and looked mightly pleased at my offer, and I then told him that if he would come into the house I would tell him exactly how I wanted the shed built; as it was, after all, cold work standing about.

When we were by ourselves I disclosed all the circumstances.   He

looked rather chapfallen when I said that it was a part of my *ruse*
to give it out I was going to make him a shed, but he took it so
well that I promised him if the plan succeeded, though I had made
the proposal partly in joke, I would carry it out in earnest. The
shelter was, to say the truth, very much needed, as Hayes was
obliged to have all his stock brought home if only moderately hard
weather set in.

That very afternoon, I met Hayes by appointment at the land
where the hangs were. He had two of his labourers with him, and
I pointed out a place at which to begin, near the corner of the field
farthest from where they were set. After half an hour's digging
we came to stone, and being apparently satisfied with that spot,
I tried again rather nearer to the required locality, and with a
favourable result. Two more holes, selected as to their position
apparently at random, seemed all that was needed to prove the
presence of stone, and I took care to have them made quite large
enough to admit a man being hid without unnecessary cramping, as
it was quite possible that the enviable possessor for the time being
of these *troux de loup* might be constrained to pass the time between
daylight and dark in the self-imposed retirement marked out for him.

Oakes expressed a wish to be the watcher, and Thornton, after
a show of resistance, gave up the post of honour to him. In
this concession our friend rather seemed to fall in with Oakes's
proposition as if he were conferring a favour on him.

After Thornton had had his tea I chanced to go out into the yard,
and saw a light in the room I had given him for a workshop; and
going upstairs I found Thornton making another dead-fall trap.
He said the reason he had come down to the house was for the
purpose of meeting Oakes, if he should chance to be about, so as to
give him a hint in watching, for want of which all our trouble might
be useless. This suggestion was to have been to the effect that he
ought not to be in the nearest hiding-place to the hangs, as it was
just possible the poacher might take a look at that one, and not
finding anyone hid, would probably not give himself the trouble of
investigating those farther away. Oakes had, however, gone home

at about five o'clock ; and although Thornton's anxieties about this matter troubled him a good deal, he resolved at last to trust to the chapter of accidents, especially as Oakes had shown he could, on occasion, display good common sense and discernment when called on to act promptly.

My chief fear was that the person, whoever he might be, who had set the hangs would not come and look at them in the morning, although the strong probabilities were that the visit *would* be paid then.

I was interrupted during breakfast the next morning by an announcement that "George wanted to see me particularly." On his entrance into the room I could at once see triumphant success in every lineament of his countenance. It seems he had been on the spot at half-past four that morning, and, not daring to show a light at that hour (although it had been safe enough to do so when he and Thornton investigated the hangs the night but one before), he *felt* for the hangs, and succeeded in finding two of the number, both of which he "ran" as before. He regretted to himself that he had not any "hare dawn" to put in the knot. Having done this, he proceeded to compress himself into the nearest pit to the hangs he had "run," and this not being more than sixty yards off, he thought himself right in every way.

"I was sitting there, sir," he said, "and thinking how nicely I should nail him, when all of a sudden it struck me, 'Suppose the feller comes and looks in.' I got up as quick as I could, and chose another hole about fifty yards further off, and piled up some little stones and bits of clay, so that I could see through 'em, and not show the top of my head. I had a terrible long time of it, and I began to think he wouldn't come, and that there I was regular fast till night. I could see day just begin to break, when all of a sudden I could hear a noise like a man's boot-toe kicking a gate, and then another noise, as if some one had jumped down on to the ground. Thinks I, 'You're here at last, my lad.' In about a minute I could see a man come up the hedge-side, and then he stopped, but not near any of the hangs. He caught sight of the holes as were made, and, after going along the hedge-side a matter of a score yards farther, he made as if he were going to the hole as I had just got out of. He turned again, however, and looked all about him, and then he starts off again for the hole, and went right up to it and looked in. I *was* some pleased as I'd not stopped in it. It were getting light pretty quick then, and it were light enough for me to see as the man were a stranger. He come to the first hang, and saw it was standing, and then to one of those as I'd run. He wouldn't touch it for two or three minutes, but at last he set it again, after looking very closely at the ground about. I had taken care to prick it pretty well, and had made a good long 'scrawt' or two, as if a hare had done it with her ' clays ' " (clays being understood by the reader uninitiated into the dialect of some of our northern provinces to mean " claws").

" I let him set this one all right, and then he came to the next as was knocked down. I guessed he'd be a bit ' brazender ' in setting this, as the other hadn't led to any damage ; so I let him alone, but just when he'd finished it, and was beginning to try with his hand whether it was the right height, I nipped softly out and got within thirty yards within him. He reared hisself up and catched a ' glint' of me, and off he went like lightning. I ' afters ' him, and *you* know, sir, they say I can run sharpish, but he was almost too many for me. Luckily, I'd the best wind of the two for keeping it up, but I couldn't just lay hold of him. I was afraid as he'd suddenly clap down and send me over him, but he didn't seem up to that, so I just put the end of my stick between his knees, and the moment it touched both knees he went over on his face and regular scraped along the ground.

" As soon as he got up I collared him, but he wouldn't give his name, and, as I told you, sir, I didn't know him, and I marches him off to Mr. Hayes' to see if he did.

" When I got down to the farm I found they knowed him there, for he'd been mending a turnip drill about a week before, and somehow had got on to that land, and seed as there were a hare or two about."

CHAPTER XII.

The Poacher known to Thornton—Walking-stick Guns—Ridding Wall for
Rabbits—The Poacher informs Thornton respecting the Air-gun—Unroosting the Pheasants—Catching the Poachers with the Air-gun.

IT was the usual custom with Thornton to come down to the
house after he had been his rounds to tell me all that had
happened during the day; and on the same evening that the
events just narrated had occurred he duly made his appearance.
I directed him to sit down and enter into any details he might have
to communicate. Having availed himself of my permission, he
proceeded as follows :

"I have been talking to George, sir, about this man he's catched,
and I am sure he's the same that I have had some trouble with
before. The description George gives of him makes it pretty certain
it can be no one else. About twenty years ago, when I was a grown
man, but not more than two-and-twenty, I was keeper under my
father at General Quentin's. We had a famous lot of game—all
pheasants, hares, and partridges. We had no grouse or black game,
but in one part there was any quantity of rabbits. In the town
near our place was a man as could do almost anything in the
joinering or whitesmithing way; he could make a chest of drawers one
day, and a gun-lock the next; nothing seemed to beat him. A very
tidy decent man he was, too, and always minded his business. He
had three lads, as was all like himself in the way of working, but
they were terrible fellows to poach. 'Lawless' their name was, and
they took after their name in every way where game was in the case.
The old man got a withered arm with laying hold of some hot sheet
lead they were rolling one day, and he never did any good after, and
only lived about two years longer. Jem, as was the eldest, went
to America ; Sam went into Wales and got regular work at some

large foundries in those parts, and Harry 'listed in the ——th, and, after being in the ranks fourteen months, was allowed to go into the armourer's workshop, where he was getting on very well. One day he was helping to move an arm chest, and the rope gave way, and the end of the chest came on his feet, and it was thought as it had broken 'em ; but it wasn't so bad as that, for it was only the small bones like as was crushed. He was in the hospital a long while, and as he seemed not to get any better, they gave him his discharge.

"I was a good bit put about when I heard as he'd come home, for I knew he'd be after poaching as soon as he was well, and we'd all hoped that when he'd once joined we'd got 'shut' of him for good.

"I dare say, sir, you've seen those walking-stick guns that go with a light charge of shot and powder ? Well, he had one of 'em, and the very first day I saw Harry when he could get about, he had it with him. It was in the Market-place where we met, and I said, ' Why, Harry, have they showed you how to make them walking-stick guns in the army ? ' He looked soft like, and said as it wasn't his, but he was going to mend it. Now, I didn't believe him, for he turned so desperate red, and I told him to mind what he was about, for poaching was sure to bring him into a mess. I asked how his feet were getting on, and he said they were stronger, but he found them ache terribly if he stood at the bench long together, and he intended going out mowing and doing a bit of harvest work that summer. I met him harvesting soon after, but not in the way he quite liked.

"It was in this way, sir. I'd gone my rounds one morning, and in a grass field above one of our woods I saw four men mowing. Says I, ' One of them's Harry Lawless ; I hope he'll keep out of mischief.' I went home to dinner, and after I'd had it I took the same beat as I'd been in the morning part ; not for any particular reason as I remember, but all the same I *did* go that beat. When I gets nearly opposite to the field where I'd seen the men, I heard them whetting their scythes. It just struck me that only *three* were whetting, and if this was so, one of 'em might have got into the wood after the rabbits. I went quietly up to the wall and looked over, and sure enough there *was* only three. I went gently on to a spot where there had been a cross fence in the wood, but it had all fallen down except in some bits of places. I now stopped to listen, and could plainly hear a noise of pulling stones out of the wall. It was luckily on the farthest side, so I crept softly up and looked over, and there was Master Harry, kneeling down, and ridding for a rabbit. After working away for at least five minutes, and feeling in every direction, he at last rises up, and wiped the dirt off his knees, and said to himself, 'Her's gone through, I fancy.' 'I think her has, Harry,' I says. O dear, sir, if you had but seen how scared he was! He begged as I'd say nothing about it, and not pull him up. I told him, 'Now, Harry, you know as my master's very particular, and if I don't inform on you he's very likely to turn me off; but look here, I'll run my chance of that if you'll promise to attend to your work, and not come bothering after the game.' He gave his word as he wouldn't, and said he shouldn't have come *then*, but they put up a young rabbit while they were mowing, and he run after it, and got to the plantation just in time to see it go into the old cross wall.

"Harry was very much obliged by my letting him off, and I took care to let the General know what I had done. He rather blamed me for not going on with it, but I told him I thought good 'ud come of it, as Harry might some day do me a good turn. I couldn't quite make my master see it, and he talked about a bird in the hand being worth two in the bush. However, he let me do as I thought right, and it came back to me in a way I certainly never could have expected.

"I'd forgot all about it, till one night in November I happened to be giving some medicine to a dog of the General's as was very ill, when a knock came at the door, and I went to open it, and there I found my friend Harry Lawless. It was a terrible wet night, and I asked him what could have brought him out. He says, 'If you don't mind my keeping you up for half an hour, I'll tell you, Thornton, what's brought me.'

"He took a seat and began. 'Do you know Turner and Joddrell,

and Elvett and Wilmot, Thornton ?'   'Know 'em,' I says ; 'like I
do ; why, they're the biggest poachers in the county.'   'So they
are,' he says, 'and it's them as I want to tell you on.   About two
months sin' two of 'em comes to me, and they says, "Can you make
a hair-gun ? "   "Like I can," I says.   "Well, then," says they, "we
wanten one with three barrels like in a ' star,' two above and one
under.   They must hold a good big shot each, about as big as a
' blacklead ' (meaning a lead pencil).   The gun must have a rattling
great globe to it, so as to send out a lot of air at a time ; and the
barrels must be spread out a bit, so as to send the bullets into a
spot about as big as your hand at a matter of six yards.   Can you
make it ? "   I tell'd 'em I could, but it 'ud cost a sight o' brass.
" How much ? " says they.   I thought a bit, and then says, "Eight
pound."   " Eight pound ! " they says ; " nought o' the sort ; why,
we could get it made in Birmingham for five."   " Well," I says,
then get it made, but don't ask me to pump it for yer."   I knowed,
you see, Thornton, as if they got it done cheap it 'ud burst.   Well,
after a great deal of bother and baiting me down, I said I'd make it
'em for seven pound ten.   They come for it about three o'clock this
afternoon, and blessed if the blackguards didn't offer me four pound !
and at last I got 'em to allow five ; but I says to myself, " I'll be
even with yer, you beggars ! "   Now look here, Thornton, you
behaved very good-natured about that rabbit, for I heard as you'd a
sore time to bring the old General round, and I says to myself, if I
can do Thornton a good turn I will.   I don't say, mind you, that I
would have told of these chaps if they'd behaved right like, but as
they have done so shabby, I've made up my mind to take it out of
'em.   They'll take the gun home and see what it'll do at a mark
first, and then you see they'll try it among the pheasants.   There's
Frank Addy 'll tell me the night they mean coming over here, and
as soon as he knows I'll incense you about it.   Mind, I can't say—
no more can Frank—whereabout they mean going.   You must have
middling of strength out that night, and run your chance of falling
in with 'em.'

    " The next morning, about ten o'clock, Harry came again, and said that that night was the one fixed for a trial of the air-gun, and consequently we were out very strong, but could making nothing of it. I had taken care to 'put down' the pheasants in every wood but one, and I was quite puzzled to know how it was they had not been. I could not go and ask Lawless, because it might get out that I was being 'put up' to something or other, and then he'd have been in a mess with the poachers, and I knew 'em to be a desperate lot, as 'ud stick at nothing if he *did* blow upon 'em.

"I'd fixed with my men where we were to meet that night, and was just getting my supper, when a knock came at the door, and in marches Harry again.

" 'Now's your time, Thornton,' he says; 'they're sure to go to-night. The reason they were not out last night was because one of 'em tried a shot with the gun, and in pumping it again (on a dusty stone, I fancy it must have been) they got a piece of grit into the valve, and it began losing air like ought, and they brought it back to me, and I was till nigh twelve o'clock last night before I could get it to hold. I know very well as they'll soon spoil it, but if it last long enough for *one* night's work it may do you a lot of damage; and I tell you this—you may depend it *shall* be made so as it shall tire 'em of it, if you and your men can't get hold of it.'

"I thanked Harry for what he had done, and what he promised to do, and gave him some whisky and water, and told him to go back home as soon as possible, so as not to be suspected.

"The pheasants had been 'put down' again, all except in one spot, and about half-past ten I started off and met our men as I had done before.

"We went and planted at the covert where the pheasants hadn't been disturbed, and there we waited till about half-past twelve. Everything was quite quiet, and we began to think they had been put off again somehow. We had a terrible big extent of woods and pheasants in all of 'em, and we thought we'd go and look in some of the other woods, as of course in unroosting the pheasants we couldn't make them *all* safe.

" We made nothing out, however, and we come back to the planting as we'd left, and I sent two of our men, named Swindells and Bentley (two rare good ones), to hearken if they could make anything out at the far side, about a quarter of a mile away.

" They come back in an hour, and said they could hear nothing, and it was getting so late in the night that I had a regular bad heart of it. We had just fixed to go home, when I fancied I heard a noise like a man knocking his hands together with gloves on. I can't think of anything else as it was just like. In three or four minutes we heard it again, quite distinct. 'Lads,' I says, 'they're here! Down!' I whispered; 'look yonder!' We could see five men coming quite plain, and all of a sudden they stopped, and off goes the air-gun again. *This* time they waited to pump again, and then they come steadily on, staring up into the trees.

" Our men were all laid flat down, and the poachers came so close on to us that one of the men (a 'very good woolled 'un,' called Allen Ryder) made a grab at the leg of the one as carried the gun, and pulled him head over heels on to the ground.

" Of course we made a rush, and all the rest cut like anything, but we had 'em in no time; we couldn't, however, find the air-gun pump anywhere. In falling down the gun itself had got strained. The barrels were all right, but the thread of the screw inside the collar of the globe had torn out. The next thing was to count up what pheasants they'd got, and would you believe it, sir, there was *sixteen* found on 'em.

" It seems (as we heard at after) they had gone to another wood and looked it through, and had got five pheasants there, and when we left the wood as we'd been tenting, they left the other, and so we'd like crossed on the road.

" We sent the rascals to the lock-up for that night, and the first thing in the morning I went with Bentley to have a look for the pump. In hunting for it we came across three more pheasants dropped in a line. Bentley says, ' Why, this is the road that chap took as I run down, but he was catched two hundred yards further.' We went to the place as near as we could judge, and sure enough there was another pheasant; so they'd got twenty in a terrible short time.

"We could not find the pump then, but about two months after I was coming through that wood, and I stumbled on the pump at least sixty yards from where the scrimmage had been. It was all eat with rust, but I brought it home as a sort of a curiosity, and I fancy Captain Quentin (that's the General's son, sir) has it now. It was a desperate good job getting the air-gun the very first night they used it.

"The old General gave Harry a five-pound note, and another five pounds among all of us; and he told me at after how glad he was I'd let Harry Lawless off in the way I did. Depend upon it, sir, it does not do to be *too particular*. When I didn't fetch the law of Harry I knew as well as he did that I could have dropped upon him heavy; but it was a good case for a keeper doing a bit of blowing up and then letting there be an end to it. You see, sir, Harry didn't forget it, and it answered to me a desperate deal better than if I'd made him pay a matter of a pound or so at the time.

"This was the first time I came across Harry about the game, and he made a good thing of it; but the next time he came off second best, as I'll tell you, sir.

CHAPTER XIII.

Mark on Poacher's Face—Shooting Hares with Walking-stick Gun—"Vision" while setting Nets—Death of Poacher—Bursting of the Stick-gun—Rabbit poaching for a coursing Match—Watching Railway Trains.

"AFTER that matter with the air-gun, sir, Harry kept very quiet, and he often told me he was sure the poachers suspected him of having told of 'em, but they never could prove anything. That they *did* suspect him was shown some few weeks after in the following way :

"Harry had received orders from a farmer to make a brand to mark his pigs with, instead of punching a little hole in the pig's ear with a saddler's punch, as was usually the practice in that part of the country. He had welded the letter 'O' on to the handle of the brand, and had just thrown it on the floor of his shop, when two of the well-known poachers came in to have a chat with him. One of them says, 'I say, Harry, what 'ud you do at a chap as blowed on his mates?' 'Well,' says Harry, 'I never knowed anyone as did, so I can't say what I'd do.' One of 'em says, 'I'd mark the beggar, that I would.' The other takes up the brand and says, 'Yes, I'd mark him like *that !*' He pushed the brand at Harry's face, but he hadn't an idea as it was burning hot, as it wasn't *red*. Harry gave a tremendous great jump, and shouted out 'Oh,' and a good deal more that I need not tell you, sir. The brand had left a great 'O' on his cheek, and being a feller with a very freckled face it turned a sort of pinkish white when it healed; but there is the mark as plain as can be, and there he'll always have it. The man as burnt him was dreadful frightened; as it was an accident, no more notice was taken of it, but Harry saw as plain as anything that they judged him about losing the air-gun.

"When George told me that the man as he'd caught had a 'O'

G

marked on his face, I knew at once it could be no one else but Lawless, especially as he was a whitesmith, but I'd no idea he was in this part of the country. I knew he had left the town where he lived when he made the air-gun, and I'll tell you, sir, what it was as drove him at last. First of all, you must know that my seeing that walking-stick gun in his hand rather put him out, as he fancied no one knew there was such things : but *I'd* known of 'em for years and years.

"One very fine summer evening I was coming home to tea, and I fancied I heard a very faint crack of a gun near what we called the warren, and where we had a good lot of rabbits. I turned back and got into the road, and in about ten minutes I met Rowley (one of our under-keepers), and I says, 'Rowley, did you hear a gun or a rifle ?' 'Yes,' he says, 'I fancied I did, and I run down to the warren, thinking it sounded there. I saw nothing but Harry Lawless coming along quite quiet like, but it wasn't him as shot, for he'd only a stick in his hand, and nought in his pockets I'm sure.' 'What sort of a stick was it ?' I asked. 'Oh, it was an ash stick, with a longish bend in the middle,' he says.

"'Now, Will.,' I says, 'it's too late I fancy to-day, but you be about the warren to-morrow at the same time, and if you meet Harry, mind you follow him. I know I've like frightened him out of *one* walking-stick gun, and I have a strongish notion that the stick as you saw was another of 'em.

"I left Rowley and turned back to go home, and all of a sudden it struck me that, as Rowley hadn't appeared to Lawless to suspect his having a gun with him (as was the fact), he might try another shot with it somewhere else. I ran as hard as ever I could, so as to get *before* Lawless on the road he seemed to be making, and I managed to hide myself in a plantation where there was a little grass field taken out for breeding our pheasants in. The field was about two acres and there was always a nice bit of grass in it, because the pheasant's food and things had, as you may say, manured the ground.

There were generally eight or ten hares or leverets feeding here, and I thought it not at all unlikely that Master Lawless might try his hand at one of 'em on his way home.

"I hadn't been hid more than some twenty minutes when I heard a stick crack somewhere behind me, but I daren't stir to look round. I was stood as close as I could get to the stem of a nice thick young spruce. In about half a minute who should come close past but young Fred. Kaye, a cousin of Harry's. He looked all about him, but by the greatest good luck did not catch sight of me. He then went to the wall of the little field, and peeped carefully over. He drew back a yard or so, and, still keeping his eyes on something in the field, he beckoned sideways with his hand. I knew at once what was coming, and sure enough Lawless joined him ; and after a bit of whispering, Kaye left his mate and disappeared round the corner. Harry had the ' bent stick ' with him, and I saw at once it was a gun. After a bit of waiting he cocked it, and then put the muzzle over the wall and raised himself slowly up. He shifted the gun quite sudden and fired. I could tell at once that he'd had to shoot at a hare as she was running instead of sitting, and *that* showed me he didn't know the proper way of shooting over a wall. I'll show you how, sir, some day. He threw the gun down, and nipped over the wall like lightning, and Kaye and him run the hare for I should think a hundred yards. They caught her at last, and killed her. She set up a terrible ' skrike.' I wouldn't have let 'em killed her, except that she'd a broken hind leg.

"I picked up the gun, and hid again behind the spruce, and over they both come, regular out of breath. Harry seemed knocked all of a heap when he did not find the gun, and I gave 'em a minute or two to look, and then I bolts out and collars him. Kaye was so frightened he couldn't stir, and I took the hare out of his hand without his offering the least resistance.

"Now, Harry, I says, ' this won't do. I let you off about that rabbit, and you said as you wouldn't come again. I doubt you are in a box *this* time.' He saw it was no good talking ; but all he asked was for the gun to be given up to him. ' No,' I says, ' I sha'n't do nothing of the sort. That gun will have to help me to tell a little story before the magistrates.' 'Well,' he says, 'then take no notice of Fred. here.' 'No,' I says, 'I must teach Fred. a lesson too.' Fred. began hollering like a great girl when I told him this; but it was no good. I was regular angry at the fellows.

"The end of it all was that they had to pay, and I was glad to find that it gave Kaye such a sickener, he never went after poaching any more. And now, sir, I must tell you what drove Lawless.

"He was out one night with a regular bad 'un of the name of Carter, and they'd got some purse nets set for hares. A hare bolts into a net as Carter was watching, and he turned to kill her, when all of a sudden he saw what he described as a bright white flame of fire in the net, that quite dazzled him! He fell down in a kind of a fit, and was so found by his companion Lawless. When Carter came round and had explained the cause of his attack, Harry tried to laugh him out of it, and said it was nought but an extra glass of rum he had had. It was all of no use. Carter went gloomily home, and said he should be dead in a day or two. In the afternoon of the following day a neighbouring blacksmith, as was going to 'ring' a cart-wheel, asked Carter to come and help him to drag some thorns to the fire. Although regular low spirited and 'down' about what he said he'd seen, he consented to help a bit, but he repeated what he'd before said about not having long to live. A very large heap of thorns lay at one end of the yard, and Carter and a man named Ward went with a couple of hayforks to bring some of them. Carter had thrown down one lot on the fire, and was leaning on his fork watching 'em burn, and thinking perhaps of the fire he fancied he'd seen the night before. Ward was bringing a forkful of thorns, and in the act of dragging them had his back to Carter. The thorns consisted of one large bough, from which a smaller one had been half split off in cutting the tree down. Ward used all his force to lift the whole lot on the fire at once, when all of a sudden the small bough split off, the fork went over his left shoulder before he could check it, and one of the 'grains' run through Carter's head, close behind one ear, coming out at the other.* The poor fellow dropped as dead as a stone, and in falling the shaft broke off close to where it joins the grains. The fork was draw'd out of Carter's head as soon as possible, and, curiously enough, not more than two or three drops of blood come.

"This ending of Harry's friend so regular upset him that he left his home ; but the very last thing he did was to give the walking-stick gun to a poaching mate as he was very thick with. It happened to be loaded when he give it him, and the poacher seeing a sparrow set on the pigstye wall, banged off at it, but never thought about the 'stop' as was in the barrel to prevent the dirt from getting in when you used it for a walking-stick, so the gun burst just against the lock and sent his left hand all to bits. The man had been a sore bad 'un, and I can't say as I cried my eyes out when I heard of it.

"I hadn't a notion what had become of Lawless, but I suppose he must be following his trade as a journeyman not far from here. The name he give to George was Job Slack, and he said he worked for Heywood, the machine-maker, at Amcoats, but I don't believe it's anyone but him himself, and if so, we shall not see him again in a hurry. George ought to have brought him here, but he didn't perhaps know quite what to do, and as he'd got his name he thought it enough. If it *is* Harry, and he bolts, it'll be the best thing after all, for I'd rather he was out of this part of the country than in it, as he can't hold off poaching."

I sent Oakes for a summons, and one was obtained, but *serving it* was a very different affair, for Mr. Lawless had retired from the scene, and left no memento of himself at his lodgings except a ball of strong string and the haft of a knife with " H. L." scratched on the valuable strip of German silver plate that adorned one side of it. At all events, these initials went far towards corroborating Mr.

---

* The above very shocking accident is true in every detail, and occurred several years ago. The names of the various persons are of course fictitious. The narrator was a boy when it happened, and saw Carter lying dead on the sofa in his working dress about an hour after the catastrophe.

Thornton's surmises, and rendered it about a matter of certainty that Harry Lawless and Job Slack were one and the same individual.

To keep up the delusion, such as it might be termed, of the holes being made for stone to build a shed from, I had the work proceeded with, and enjoined the very strictest secrecy on my tenant Hayes, as it was just possible some similar plan might have to be adopted at a future time, and nothing would be gained by letting it be known that these holes had been made for the purpose of watching a poacher.

December and January had now passed over without any incident calling for particular remark as concerned our preserving. One morning, in the early part of February, I received a note from Arden asking me to be good enough to lend him my two men to help on an occasion when he (Arden) was likely to receive the visit of a large gang of poachers. It seems there was to be a "rabbit running" at a town about fifteen miles off, and, owing to the great facilities afforded by the railway, it was by no means improbable that his manor would be selected as the ground to get the rabbits from.

Arden, having generally a good number of men under him, had not taken the precaution that we had in the matter of guarding his fields by posts and rails, &c., although he had put any quantity of the tight wires down in his coverts.

As no dogs would probably be brought by the poachers, it was natural to expect the deficiency would be supplied by an extra number of men to "drive."

I wrote to Arden to accord my full consent to Thornton and Oakes going, and merely wished him to give what notice he could of the day (or rather night) that he would want their services.

Three days after I received a second note to say that, from all he could make out, the coursing would take place the next day; and as it was a *sine quà non* that the rabbits should be fresh caught, so as not to get cramped and stiff, he should be glad if I would send the two men at once.

It was only three miles to Arden's house, so my keepers left about seven o'clock in the evening. I waited most patiently for the next morning to arrive, but it was towards the middle of the afternoon before Thornton and Oakes returned.

My first inquiry naturally was, " Well, Thornton, did they come ? "

" O yes, sir," he said, " they come safe enough."

" Well," I said, " and how was it ? "

" Why, when we got to Arden's, sir," he said, " we found he'd had to send for more men than he'd thought of at first, for from what had been told him there was very little doubt the poachers 'ud be at his place that night, and a terrible strong lot too. We had, however, seven of Arden's men — counting him in — George and me, and four of Mr. Reynardson's. As the poachers were sure to bring a great lot of tackle with 'em, they most likely wouldn't give it up without a 'rally.' All the keepers had got their ' beehive ' hats on, so as not to mind a goodish crack on the head. George and me crammed a lot of ' hards ' into ours, and we all tied our hats tight under our chins ; and Arden's missis sewed a band of white linen about six inches wide round *both* of our arms, not round *one* only.

" While we were thus occupied a lad of Arden's arrived from the station, where he had been watching the trains. He said that by the six o'clock train there were three men came that no one could doubt were regular poachers, and that eight more got out who looked like mill-hands or stockingers, but that none of them seemed to notice each other. ' That's them, for a thousand,' Arden said. The lad mentioned the fact that they had no sacks or hampers of any sort with them. ' No,' said Arden, ' not likely ; they've got all the tackle ready for 'em a day or two back, and they know well enough where to fetch it from. But, come lads, it's time we were moving.' We had about half a mile to go before arriving at the ground where the poachers would make their attempt, if they came at all, and on our way, we fell in with two men, who turned out to be Birks (keeper to Lord Danby), and Handley, a young farmer as was very fond of going out with the keepers, like George here used to be.

" Birks had also had the trains watched, and had no doubt that the men as had been seen were those we expected.

CHAPTER XIV.

Arrangements to capture Poachers—Working with the Wind—"Trap" to deceive Poachers—Throwing Stones—Capture of Poachers and Nets by Keepers and also by Police—Curious Instance of taking a "long Net"—Carrion-Crows—How to shoot over a Wall—Pulling out old Magpie and Crow's Nests.

"BIRKS's man had taken desperate good care to send one of his friends to watch a station about two or three miles off, and he came back and told him that at least five more rough-looking strangers had landed themselves in these parts. Whether or no they all belonged to the gang of poachers, as we expected, of course we couldn't speak to, but the chances were that a biggish lot 'ud be out.

"The whole of the keepers and tenters were now ready, and we moved off down the field, so as not to be seen if any people came along the footpath, though it wasn't very likely, at that time of night.

"There was a barn about a hundred yards away, and we all went in there to settle how we should work it.

"Arden had a strongish idea that the first set 'ud be along a gorse cover that was planted on the top of a hill. It was about a quarter of a mile long, or a bit longer, and I should say three hundred yards across. On one side of it there was an immense great open field, and on the lowest side a lot of nice little inclosures. In the large field the gravel had been dug for a good many years ago, and in one part there was a regular quarry as come within, I should think, a matter of half a dozen yards of the gorse cover. The cover was fenced off by a low wall as went all round it.

"Arden told me as the gorse wasn't the best rabbit ground he had ; but all the same there was a rare lot in it he said. He fixed for us to watch that cover, because the large quarry field was a famous set for a lot of long nets.

"We started in about ten minutes, and got to the place, and it was then about half-past ten or so. We clapped down in the nearest corner, so as to be right for 'em coming on account of the wind. We had just fixed to divide a bit, when Birks, who was looking out with his night glass, says, 'I see 'em!' By some clumsy management they had come into the field *up the wind*. Birks says, 'I see about a score or so, and they're beginning to run the net out.' I should think they weren't above ten minutes before they had it all set, and they finished pegging within four yards of where we were hid. One man stopped at our end, and waited for a rabbit coming in, and we could just see most of the others beating. At first only about a dozen started out, but at last they were most of 'em a-gate, and the man as was at our end went away too, on purpose to help. We couldn't make it off anyhow—not a rabbit come in. We made sure now that something had put the rabbits in, and, if this was so, the poachers 'ud take up the nets and be off for another set at Arden's best spot.

"The wall was so low that we couldn't creep up to get among the thick of 'em; and although we could nail the man as 'ud come to take up the net, yet that wouldn't be enough for us, and we were regular puzzled. All of a sudden Birks says, 'I'll draw 'em!' and he got over the wall, keeping himself flat on his chest, and crawled to the net. We saw him put his hand up to the top of the nearest peg, and then crawl off to the quarry hole about six yards away. In about a second we saw the peg shake, and a man came running quite light like along the net. He came close to us and waited, and then went back again. In about ten minutes he came again, and again he goes back. Arden whispered, '*I* see how he's worked it—he's got a string to the net to draw 'em.' Sure enough it wasn't long before several of 'em comes running altogether down to where we was hid, and we could see how regular 'done' they were. All of a sudden Arden cries out, 'Now, lads!' and *in* we goes at 'em. One of the poachers gave a great whistle on his fingers, and we saw

some of 'em come running up. Those as were near us jumped back
a few yards. I knew what it was for, and shouted out, 'Look out—
stones.' Every man of us ducked down, and the stones went right
over us. We didn't give 'em time to send any more, but tackled
'em at once. Six were inclined to make a stand, but the others cut
as quick as they could. We fairly nailed four out of the six, and
then we looked after the net. Birks and Rowley and me all set off
to the far end of the line of nets, but we were too late to save it all.
We couldn't say how much they had taken, but we judged it to be
about 150 yards as was gone. We found 300 yards standing.
Altogether we made a very good night's work of it, but Arden was
desperate put about as he hadn't got all the net, and he could do
nothing but grumble all the way home. You see, sir, the poachers
stood long enough to give one of their mates a chance to save the
net farthest away, and he *did* save it for a bit.

"It was a very sharp dodge of Birks to keep shaking the net, as
we couldn't have got so many men together, if he hadn't done so.

"We took those as we'd catched to Arden's house, and sat up
with 'em all night. About breakfast time a little girl came up to
the cottage to say her father would be glad if Arden would step as
far as his house as he wanted to see him. The man who sent the
message was a rural policeman. Arden accompanied the little girl,
and came back in about half an hour, looking desperate pleased.
'Well,' he says, 'you chaps (meaning the poachers) are out of luck,
for the police have dropped on your mate with the net!' With all
sitting up together we'd got quite friendly like, and the poachers
was chaffing Arden about losing part of the net. They *did* look
vexed when Arden told 'em what he'd heard!"

Thornton was very warm in praise of the inventive genius of
Birks, and spoke of him as a "very deep little fellow;" and so, in
fact, he had shown himself to be, as it would have been difficult to
catch more than one of the poachers if he had not hit upon that
scheme.

It seems that the expedition was under the guidance of five very
notorious and experienced poachers, and the extra hands they had

brought were, as they appeared to be, stockingers and mill-hands, who would do to "drive" the ground as well as anyone.

I was told shortly afterwards that the reason no rabbit was caught was explained by the fact that the village surgeon had been his round and made a short cut across the large open field, and so had, unintentionally, done a considerable amount of good.

While upon the subject of long netting, Thornton told me a very curious circumstance that happened on a manor adjoining to the one where he had been keeper before engaging himself with me. It was as follows: One of the under keepers was looking the coverts round early one morning, and to his great astonishment found about 250 yards of long net set. As he could neither hear nor see any person about, and could not in the least tell what to make of it, he waited about for at least an hour, and then came to the conclusion that he might as well collect the netting and make off with it, and this he did.

More than two years passed, and one night a capture of poachers and nets was made on this very property; and the poachers had shown a considerable amount of fight previously to three of them being secured. Two of the keepers were much injured, and the facts all coming out well at the assizes, all of the three were sentenced to fourteen years' transportation. The under-keeper who had found the first lot of long netting, was also called as a witness in the second case, and when it was all over, one of the poachers asked if he might be permitted to see the keeper, as he had something to communicate to him.

Leave was given to him to do so, and a day fixed at the gaol. At the time appointed, the keeper waited on the poacher, by the authority of an order from one of the visiting magistrates, and, having been shown into the cell where he was confined, received from that worthy a full account of the reason for leaving out the netting.

It seems that the gang to which this poacher belonged had made arrangements to set the side of that covert, and had in fact just got the nets all down. They had not turned the dogs out, but were about doing so when they perceived a very strong body of men coming quietly through the gate within fifty yards of them. Not being themselves very strong that night—seven men only being out —they did not venture to wait the attack of such a body of *keepers* as they imagined them to be.

The supposed keepers, on their part, were in fact another gang of poachers from a town about six miles off, and they, seeing the poachers standing close together, at once arrived at the conclusion that they must be the keepers. Acting upon this mistaken impulse, the two gangs retreated as fast as they could, leaving the nets to fall into the hands of one of the under-keepers, as I have shown.*

I had now formed a regular habit of going round the property as much in the capacity of keeper as landlord, and one day I took a stroll, with a double-gun on my arm, to look at some traps I had set. I was resting on a stile when Thornton happened to come up, and I remained talking to him for a considerable time. The winter had now passed, and we had every promise of an early and fine spring. I had seen a couple of carrion-crows about, and so had my keeper, and it was evident enough they were on the look-out for a nesting place. We were talking about them, when Thornton suddenly remarked, " Why, them's the two carrion-crows yonder, sir ! " Certainly, what appeared to be crows were visible in a large grass field nearly half a mile off. We took out our glasses, and soon were convinced of the fact. " Now, sir," said Henry, " you will be pretty sure to get a shot if you like to try, for they're in a niceish spot for getting to. All you must do will be to mind they do not see you going along the wall-side, and when you get near to the spot they're at——" I stopped Thornton by suggesting that he would do it much better than myself, and so I gave him my gun and told him to try. He at once started off, and began by making a considerable *détour*, so as to get to the end of the wall down which it was his intention to make an approach.

He succeeded in reaching this point, and then he commenced creeping along under the wall, stopping occasionally to look through

---

* The above curious incident actually happened a few years ago.

some interstice or other between the stones. I had my glass on him all the time, and so could observe every movement. One of the carrion-crows was apparently about fifty yards from the wall, and the other a good deal nearer to it. I saw by Thornton's proceedings that he was within shot, and now I observed him turn round so as to have his left side to the fence. He then put the gun to his shoulder and aimed, as I thought, at something on the ground. In a second he sprang up, swept the gun over the wall, and bang went the first barrel at the carrion-crow farthest from him, before it had time to get on the wing. It was very pretty to see how clean he killed the other before it had gone ten yards. It shut-to its wings and dived head-first down, and bounced nearly a foot off the ground. The first one was, it seems, a very long way off, and, being only winged, had made off across the field, but was soon caught.

When Thornton joined me I bestowed considerable commendation on the manner in which he had manœuvred. " I thought," said I, " that you had seen a stoat or a weasel come out of the wall, when you appeared to aim at something on the ground." " Ah ! you saw me, sir ! " said Henry. " What I did *then* was part of my usual way of shooting over a wall. Now, sir, if you put the gun-muzzle over first, and then follow it, as one may say, with your head, and try to get a sight, it is ten to one that any shy bird, like a carrion-crow, sees the first ' glint,' and away he goes. Now, if you have the gun to your shoulder, and then spring suddenly up and ' sweep ' it over, all you have to do is to pull the trigger. I saw that the farthest carrion-crow was about fifty yards off, and I didn't think I should kill her ; but all the same she was in more danger than me, and as it turned out I winged her. I then had lots of time for the other with the second barrel." " Yes," I said, " and very clean you killed her."

" By the bye, sir," said Thornton, " now the weather is fine and dry, it would be as well to go through all the Scotch and larch plantations, and pull out any old carrion-crow or magpie's nests there are. I know, indeed, of a good lot, and if we don't pull them out it will rather bother us, as we shan't know old 'uns from new.

Hadn't I better get Tom Wood and a ladder, and have 'em done before any rain comes and wets the trees again? It's terrible mauling work for clothes when they're *dry;* but when they're *wet* it's almost impossible to go up 'em."

I told him to procure the services of the individual alluded to, a very sharp little fellow, who could turn his hand to anything, and who had Oakes's fondness for occasional tenting and keepering. He was also handy at climbing trees.

The next morning we started off for the larch plantation, which had been the scene of our exploit in the previous October, and there we met Wood. Thornton had provided himself with a light ladder, about fourteen feet long, and a garden fork. The latter implement he assured me was just the thing for destroying magpie nests. If you get within a yard or so of the nest and thrust the grains of the fork into it, and rest the cross handle against your right shoulder, you can lift the whole affair out at once; whereas if you pull it with your hands it can only be got out stick by stick, and being in a great measure composed of thorns you scratch yourself all to pieces in the operation. People who have never been up to a magpie nest would be rather astonished at the great size of it. It would take a wheelbarrow to hold a common-sized one, and there is generally about half a stone of clay used for the foundation of the nest previously to putting in the lining.

The ladder we found a great assistance, as it enabled Wood to reach any of the lower boughs, when it was afterwards all plain sailing. Wood, although a good swarmer, was glad to have the ladder, as nothing "takes it out of you" more than swarming, if ever so accustomed to it.

By six o'clock we had pulled out as many as a score nests, and had nearly finished the plantation. From my property having been unpreserved for a few years previously, the magpies had increased very much.

CHAPTER XV.

Trees built in by Carrion-Crows and Magpies, and their Localities—Time of Day chosen for building—Rooks building and repairing Nests—Analogy between Carrion-Crow and Hare in Habit—Sparrowhawk's Nest—Habits of Hawk —Habits of Eagles — Squirrels' Nests — Climbing-irons — Circumventing " tickle " Carrion-Crows.

In three days we had pulled out every magpie nest we could find, and we then turned our attention towards the old nests of carrion-crows.　For these we looked through the Scotch and spruce plantations, and found a greater difficulty in discerning the nests than we had amongst the larch.　Carrion-crows build mostly in Scotch fir, at the very top of the tree, where the branches spread out and form a hollow that might appear almost to be made on purpose.　Although a carrion-crow nest is a tolerably large-sized affair (being about fifteen inches across), yet it is very easily missed by any person hunting for it.　At the top of a very lofty Scotch fir, and in the position I have named, it may either escape notice altogether, or else be set down as the nest of the missel thrush. The nest is, however, frequently built against the main stem of the fir, and is invariably large when so placed, and easy to see.　It will be found that if constructed on the small branches first alluded to that the stem or leader of the tree has perished and decayed away.

Another fact may also be noted, which is, that you very seldom find a carrion-crow build more than a hundred and fifty, or at the most a couple of hundred yards, from the boundary fence of any plantation.　I was indebted to Thornton for this piece of information.　It may be accounted for, perhaps, on the principle that the old bird has not to take an unnecessarily long flight before getting to the open fields where her food is.　A magpie, however, will build in the middle of the most extensive larch plantation just as soon as she will near the edge; and it is really wonderful to think how they should unerringly find the tree again that they have once fixed to build in, when there are hundreds of thousands perhaps composing the wood in which the nest is to be.

Thornton gave me a few rather interesting particulars about the habits of very wild and suspicious birds, such as carrion-crows and magpies, when building. He had, as he stated, only seen a pair of crows actually engaged in building, *once*.

They commence almost before daylight, and work away for about an hour and then stop for the day. A nest generally takes from four to six days building. In a country that admits of it, the foundation and sides are composed of old dead shanks of heath that will turn the edge of any knife unless artistically held when attempting to cut through one of them. On the top of this foundation is the lining, which is usually, if not always, cowhair. Rooks, on the contrary, though so much resembling carrion-crows, except in the colour of the bill, build their nests of the small boughs of hard-wood trees, such as elm, and these they break off by bending them backwards and forwards in a most persevering manner. The lining of a rook's nest is in nine cases out of ten composed of leaves, and the oak, it may usually be noticed, seems the favourite leaf.

Carrion-crows never by any chance use the same nest twice, and it is needless to observe that rooks will continue the old one as long as they live, and return in October to patch it up before the heavy winter's storms try it, as they might, beyond endurance.

Carrion-crows, when either building or feeding their young ones, always enter the plantation in a manner calculated to deceive any person watching them. The crow will usually settle on an outside tree in the first instance, about three hundred yards or more from the parallel line of the one in which her nest is. She then flies off to another a good way in, and then having settled for a few moments, gradually edges to the tree in which the nest is, making perhaps four separate flights altogether. Our very domestic friends, the rooks, on the other hand, court observation in every way, and most interesting it is to watch them at work—many instances having been noticed of

two rooks being occupied in carrying a stick that has proved
too large for the exertions of one only. In these latter cases,
however, it has always happened that the stick has only to be
carried a very short distance, and where the absence of the
second of a pair of rooks has not been of consequence for a
minute or two. A prolonged absence would result in the loss
of some particularly eligible piece of timber from the nest itself,
for a rookery is not to be instanced as a colony of *very* honest
people.

I suggested to the keeper that there might be some analogy
between a carrion-crow building not far from the edge of a plantation, and a hare sitting as she usually does within twenty or
thirty yards of a fence, and the larger the field, the nearer to the
fence. Thornton said, that no doubt in the case of a hare, it was
meant to make the fence a sort of refuge, as she would be over or
through it in a second or two, and a dog, if in pursuit, would be
temporarily baffled.

We had worked hard at the old nests, when we came to a patch of
very fine spruce firs, and Wood detected what he said was a carrion-
crow's nest, a good height up one of them. "No," said Henry, "that's
a sparrow-hawk nest." I was rather sceptical about it, and gave
Tom directions to pull the nest out entire if he could. In about
five minutes he descended the tree with it in his arm, and then I
perceived at once that it was not what Wood had suggested. "I
knew, sir," said Thornton, "that Tom and me was both right.
This belongs to a sparrowhawk, but it has been built on an old
carrion-crow nest. It is twice as wide as it was when first made,
and the hollow is not near so deep as the carrion-crow had it. The
sides are flattened out like, for six inches all round. This is to
allow of small birds, and mice, and those sort of things to rest upon
it without rolling off, while the old birds pull 'em to pieces before
they give 'em to the young ones. They always pluck small birds
on the nearest wall or large stone they see handy after they've
caught 'em, and then take 'em to the nest. You never by any chance
find any feathers about a sparrowhawk's nest. If there was, it 'ud

H

show anyone whereabouts the nest was fixed. They give the young hawks mice pulled to pieces, but without taking the skin off. When the young 'uns throw up the hair and small bones in a sort of hard pellet, the old hawks fly off with it and drop it a goodish way off." I asked Thornton how it was, then, that hawks should take such precautions to prevent any litter about that should betray the whereabouts of their nest, when eagles, which are of the same tribe, invariably take their food to the nest just as caught, and pluck and otherwise prepare it when there. The answer seemed reasonable enough, and it was to the purport that eagles usually build in very high and comparatively inaccessible rocks, and were prepared for the fact of the locality of their nest being discovered, but they could afford this inconvenience in knowing that the fortunate discoverers were no nearer possession than before, and that the young eagles might waste their food with perfect impunity. Now in the case of small hawks that build in trees, the only chance they have of rearing their family consists in keeping the domicile private, as discovery must lead to spoliation.

In the course of our proceedings we came across numbers of squirrel nests. These are made in the form of a round ball, and are placed against the stem of a fir a good height from the ground. The outside is composed of thin twigs, and the lining is moss and hair; a hole on one side admits the ingress and egress of the squirrel, and a most comfortable affair the nest is. I would not have any of these pulled out, as the squirrels are so comparatively harmless; I say comparatively, because they pull the buds and new shoots off spruce firs, and so may be said to do injury—but they were quite welcome to commit such depredations as far as my own property was concerned.

While we were occupied with pulling out the nests, Wood made the remark that he had been up many of these trees before, but had always had "climbing-irons" on. He showed them to me a few days after, and I found they consisted of a sort of steel stirrup, with a hollow to allow of the sole of the boot to fit in, and continued up the ancle with a bar made to accommodate itself to the

shape of the leg, and reaching about eight inches high. Through
the top end was a small oblong hole for a strap, and another lower
down, with another strap, something on the principle of a skate
fastening. The iron was made with a short stiff point, about the
size of a fowl's beak, but forged like a chisel. With the aid of these
irons Wood told me he could go up the tallest and smoothest trees
with great ease, but when amongst the boughs they were very much
in the way.

Our occupation induced several anecdotes from our companion as
to instances of "tickle" carrion-crows that had been circumvented
in spite of all their dodges by a previous keeper on the estate, who
appeared, from Wood's account, to have been very well up in vermin
trapping. For instance, we came to a Scotch fir that had a nest in
it that had become green underneath from age : " Ah ! it was here,
sir," he said, " that Groves (the former keeper) and me come round
a old carrion-crow as we thought 'ud beat us. She was sitting very
deep, we guessed, but somehow she wouldn't stay for us to get to
the tree, but she always went off when we was about sixty or eighty
yards from her. We tried her in all sorts of weather, but it was no
good, and Groves was terrible afraid as she'd forsake altogether. One
day, he says to me, ' Tom, I'll tell you how I think we can manage
her. I'll stop at the nest, and do you go out of the planting and
see where she is, and if you see her, mind you show that you've got
a gun with you.' Well we went that very same afternoon, and it
come on a nasty sort of a rain. We were looking sharp out, and
sure enough off she goes, like she'd always done before. I went
straight out of the planting, and made across yon field (pointing to
one of the adjacent inclosures) and I very soon catched sight of her
set on the top of that larch against the old drinking trough. She
was a matter of four or five hundred yards off, and I kept going
right on, but I was looking at her out of the corner of my eye all
the while. At last she took a start and settled again about a
hundred yards nearer. By that time I'd got to the field wall, and I
got over and then clapped down to see what she'd do next. Well,
off she starts again and settled about half way to the spot where I

knew the nest was. It was raining very hard all the time, and I knew she didn't like to be away for long. The next flight she made was within about twenty yards of it, and I knew she'd drop down and make for it among the boughs of the trees. All of a sudden up she gets and made as if she was going right back again, but she hadn't got more than five yards when I saw her shut her wings and drop—the next instant I heard bang! I got up to the nest and found six eggs in, just ready to hatch, and I can see the marks of the climbing-irons on the tree now, sir."

Thornton applauded Groves's knowledge of his business, and told us how he himself had been driven to exercise his powers in much the same way. As the system may be useful, I do not hesitate to explain what he did. He had found a carrion-crow's nest, and the old bird was sitting pretty deep. The plantation had been a good deal thinned, and he could not approach the nest without being observed. Waiting, as Groves had done, for a wet day, he went and put the carrion-crow off, and then climbed up to the nest and pulled out all the undermost sticks, leaving through to the lining a hole about the size of his hand. He then tied his gun to a tree about half a dozen yards off, with the sight taken fairly for the hole. He tied the trigger back to the guard, and having cut a little bit of stick, just the length between the face of the hammer and the top of the cap, he propped the hammer on full cock. He had a piece of string about sixty yards long tied to the stick, and then he went and hid behind a tree farthest away from the point where he knew the old carrion-crow was waiting. In about ten minutes he saw her come and settle a long way off, and at last she came within a few yards of the nest. He dared not look any longer, as she might in her last flight catch sight of him, so he allowed her at least another ten minutes and then pulled the string on speculation. He had taken the precaution to load with a green cartridge, and when he went to the spot he could neither see nor hear anything, so he climbed up the tree again, and surely enough he had killed the carrion-crow as dead as a stone. The plan of tying back the trigger and propping up the hammer is the simplest of all, and yet we read in accounts of bear shooting in India and other countries that a string is tied *to the trigger* and continued in the direction wished; whereas, if the other plan occurred to the mind of anyone setting a gun, it surely would always be adopted.

CHAPTER XVI.

Trapping Carrion-Crows and Magpies with Eggs—Thornton detects Footsteps
of Poacher in Grass—Shooting Carrion-Crows—" Calling "—Identification
of Poacher who made Footmarks—Dog running against Wire.

WE had now finished the whole of the plantations, and were quite
ready for the arrival of any fresh carrion-crows or magpies. It
soon became evident that we had not destroyed all these depredators.
Seldom a day passed without our seeing several of them, and as
Thornton was not partial to too much firing of guns, especially at
this time of the year, the only mode of keeping their numbers down
was by trapping or poisoning.

I kept a good number of fowls at the house, and amongst them
were a few bantams. I had pigeons also in considerable quantities.
Thornton came one afternoon to beg a few eggs for baits, and being
curious to learn how he set his traps for the crows and magpies, I
arranged to take a walk with him and observe the process.

The bantams had already commenced laying, and I had no
particular object in keeping their eggs; so, as Henry expressed a
decided preference for them over common hens' eggs, I at once told
him to get what he required.

Having obtained about half a dozen, he proceeded to boil them,
and threw into the water about a tablespoonful of coffee. This, he
told me, was for the purpose of rendering the eggs as nearly as
possible the colour of pheasants' eggs.

We went up into Thornton's workshop and selected a few steel
traps and a spade, and by Thornton's request I took with me a sheet
or two of writing paper.

Having arrived at the fields adjoining the larch plantation, the
keeper looked about for a piece of very slanting ground facing the
trees, and then proceeded to cut a square space out, about eight

inches deep at the farthest end, and coming level at the front. He then dug out a shape for the trap, and put a little grass at the farthest end of the aperture, and on the grass he deposited one of the eggs.

The trap being neatly set and covered in the place made for it, the keeper pegged down a bit of the white paper about a foot off. He set three more in the same way in other parts of the adjoining fields.

Our attention was then directed to the stream of water (which I have before alluded to as running through my property), as Thornton had decided to set a trap or two for the carrion-crows. His mode of proceeding was as follows : a small promontory of turf being found, reaching into the water, a hollow place for a trap was cut out of it, and a large sod placed in the water about six inches from the trap, and one of the eggs placed upon it, with a little bit of wet clay under the egg to form a sort of bed, which would prevent the wind blowing it off. I arranged with my keeper to accompany him in the morning when he looked at these traps. It was very early when Thornton threw a few stones up at my bedroom window, and, being a cold frosty day, I felt only half inclined to turn out ; but it would not do to make such an appointment and not keep it.

I found Henry waiting, with his gun reared up near him, and off we set. Our road lay in the direction of the large wood where the pheasants were, and the first quarter of a mile we kept the public road. Parallel with the wood, Thornton stopped, and went up to a gate, and looked over it.

"What is it, Thornton ? " I inquired.

"Look here, sir," he answered ; "there's been somebody over here, and up the hedge-side and back again. We shall find a trap up yonder, sir, or a hang or two, I expect."

It certainly did look very suspicious ; there were marks in the frosted grass where some person had evidently been.

"The worst of it is," said Henry, "the man's been so lately, that I shouldn't wonder if he's watching us *now*."

"What are we to do?" said I.

"Oh, we must go forrard with it now, sir. If he's seen us stop and look over, he knows very well it's all up; and if *he hasn't*, it's right, so I'll go and make out all about it."

Thornton jumped over the gate, and went up the hedge-side for a long way. He then got over, and proceeded about a hundred yards farther. I saw he stopped here, and looked at the ground for a few minutes, and then went on about forty yards, and again inspected the ground. I observed he went no farther, but took a short cut back to where I was standing.

"Well, Thornton, what's it all about?"

"Traps, sir; two of 'em; I see who it is plain enough. He'd a clog on, and a band" (*Anglicè*, string) "tied round his knees. He fell in jumping over the ditch (where you saw me get through that hedge), and lit on his right knee; and there's the mark of the band, and there's also the toe of his clog, as plain as can be, in the hedge where he sprinted off."

"Well," said I, "I only wish I knew who it is."

"If you'd like to see him, sir," said Henry, "I'll show him you before noon to-day."

"You don't mean it!" I exclaimed; "that *would* be capital!"

I pressed him to give me all his reasons for knowing it was the man he suspected, but he would not commit himself to *a certainty*, and evaded my cross-examination as well as he could; so I relinquished the conversation.

A short cut across some fields brought us to the place where our traps were, and in one of them we found a magpie, and a jackdaw in another. Having set them again, we went to look at the carrion-crow traps, and long before we reached the spot where they were set, no doubt existed in our minds as to the success we had met with, for five old carrion-crows were collected, and a most tremendous noise they were making.

"Aye, it's just as I thought, sir," observed Henry, "and that's why I brought the gun. Now, if you'll stop here a bit, sir, I'll cut round and get into the spinney, and I'll be bound when they see you they 'll make for them trees ; but we must keep down just now till I can get away without being seen." I promised to do all I could in the way of helping, and agreed to allow him a quarter of an hour to get round. I noticed that every minute the carrion-crows seemed less noisy, and one or two of them in fact flew right away, but returned in a short time to assist at the disturbance.

Being now pretty sure that the keeper had succeeded in reaching the little wood, I showed myself. The effect was at once apparent in the whole lot taking flight, and going, as I feared they would, quite in the wrong direction.

One of them suddenly turned aside, and after making a considerable round, went and settled on the top of one of the trees in the very wood where Thornton was concealed.

"Confound it!" I inwardly said to myself ; "why doesn't he shoot?"

The carrion-crow, after sitting perfectly silent for a few seconds, suddenly got up and flew rapidly about, making more noise than ever. What could be the matter? Two more of the lot soon returned, and joined in the row. All at once I saw one shut his wings and drop, and half a second after another did the same, and the sounds, "Bang, bang!" accounted pretty clearly for this performance. The third carrion-crow instantly removed himself from the scene of danger, and yet somehow he could not altogether leave it, but still kept flying round, though at a very great height, and making no noise at all.

I could not help thinking that at times he came almost near enough for a chance shot to reach him, but I could not at all account for his remaining about the spot. I watched him a long time, and at last saw him throw himself rapidly back with a few quick movements of the wings, and then I heard "Bang!" No, he's not touched, but, by Jove, he'd a narrow squeak for it! What's that? Why, he's *down*, surely! In a much shorter time than it takes to relate, he twisted over and disappeared, and then I heard the second barrel.

In five minutes I saw Henry emerge from the wood with a great black bundle in his hand, which it was soon evident was composed of the three carrion-crows.

It seems he saw that odd one come in first, and she was quite within reach, but instead of knocking her over he began calling, and thus induced her to make the disturbance she had done; and the consequence was that two of the others returned to assist at the fresh alarm, and gave him a beautiful right-and-left, which opportunity he at once availed himself of. The other carrion-crow very naturally took the alarm, for the neat right-and-left had acted as a "caution;" but, as she had not as yet *seen* Thornton, she could not tear herself away. Finding that the mode of calling he had adopted would not draw her within reach, he tried the stoat-call, and had the satisfaction of observing that she certainly seemed to come nearer than before. Several times he had been on the point of trying a long shot, but he was so afraid of missing, that he as often forebore to shoot. At last she seemed within possible distance, and he gave her a loose charge of No. 4, but, as I had observed, she escaped it. The other barrel was loaded with a green cartridge, and down she came. The curious part of it was that half the wing fell separate from the carrion-crow itself, and she in fact was not otherwise touched with a single grain, which shows that the cartridge had "balled." Thornton told me he had had them by him for several years, and that *old* cartridges were apt to do it.

On coming to the trap we found, as we had expected, a carrion-crow in it, and we had thus disposed of four of them in a very short time.

I had a friend staying with me a few days after this performance. He was a great whist player, but not much of a sportsman. On telling him of Thornton's judicious management, he said it was just like "holding ace, knave, and two or three trumps besides, and allowing adversaries to make their king, so as to come down on queen with ace and command the suit." He meant that if Thornton had nailed "the king" (the odd carrion-crow), he would not have got the two others. (But this *par parenthèse.*)

I was not sorry to make my way home to breakfast after our early morning's sport, and Thornton asked me if I should like to go and look at some more traps in the course of the day. I agreed to do so, and consequently about ten o'clock I joined him in the yard, and we started.

This time he took the direction of the gravel pits belonging to the township, and there we found a cart standing, and a man loading gravel into it. Thornton accosted him with, "Now, Joe!" and received the usual reply to this greeting of "Now."

After a few minutes' talk on things in general, we left the quarry. As soon as we had got a few dozen yards away, I remarked, "Why, Thornton, that's——"

"Ah! I know what you're going to say, sir," said he; "that's the man as set the traps."

"To be sure," I replied, "he's got clogs on, and string tied round his knees."

"It was for the purpose of showing him to you, sir, that I brought you round here," said Henry; "but I can't think what's set Joe on poaching, unless it's that rascal of a Dick Scourfield, and I know there's nothing *he* wouldn't do to fit us out for catching him; and then your turning him out of the farm, sir, has made him desperate savage. I've been looking for his burnin' the moor some day; and if it wasn't for these frosty nights and mornings, I'm sure he'd do it. Now this young fellow, Joe Ferrier, has always been a decent, harmless sort of a man, and I am very sorry to find as he's going wrong."

"Well, Thornton," I said, "you must watch those traps, and if you succeed in catching him, I will turn it over in my mind what to do."

We now made straight off in the direction of the large wood, which we entered at one corner. About a couple of hundred yards on we came to a dead-fall trap, out of which Thornton took a small weasel. While he was setting the trap again, I caught sight of a snap-dog, which was running a hare as hard as ever he could go, in the direction of the wood. The hare made three or four wonderfully quick turns, just in time to prevent being caught, and it was then evident she would enter the covert close to us. To our intense chagrin we had brought no gun with us, and although the meuse that the hare was making for would act as a sort of check for an instant upon the dog, yet it was a toss-up if she escaped. We shouted and clapped our hands, but it had not the slightest effect, with the exception of causing the hare to change her direction a little further from where we stood. The dog was evidently determined not to be put off. Another second, and the hare dashed through the meuse, and the dog flew over the wall and alighted within a yard of her! We gave it up as being all over, when suddenly the dog turned a splendid somersault, and came down on his back about a dozen feet off. He picked himself up, and commenced a solo of " Yo-o-o! yo-o-o! yo-o-o!" in most energetic style. " Come on, sir," cried Henry, " we can catch him." We tried all we could, but the brute was not so badly lamed as all that came to ; and after a few supplementary yells he managed to get away. Most fortunately, one of Thornton's wires had happened to be in the way, and he had gone straight on to it. We went back to look at the spot. A piece of hair and skin, about the size of a shilling, lay close to the wire, and we found it by noticing where some more hair was sticking on to it.

CHAPTER XVII.

Thornton catches the Poacher ("Ferrier")—He is cautioned, and set at Liberty —Firing the Moor—Ferrier assists in putting it out—Informs of Scourfield and McDonough—Conviction and Penalty for burning—Ferrier rewarded.

I DID not anticipate that Thornton would have very great difficulty with Joe Ferrier, as he was not, it would seem, a regularly experienced poacher; but I was at the same time anxious to learn the result. It did not, therefore, very much surprise me when a servant came in at breakfast time to announce, "Please, sir, Thornton wants to see you." Having given orders for that gentleman to be shown in, he duly made his appearance.

"Well, Thornton, what have you done?" I inquired.

"Oh, I got him, sir, and he's in the kitchen now; and terribly ' off ' he is about it. I never saw a man so regular done as he was; and now he wants to see you, sir, to try and get you to look over it."

"But how did you catch him?" I asked.

"Why, sir, I was there a goodish bit before daylight, and took care to get to the spot from the other side, instead of going through the gate out of the road. I knew very well he'd come that way, and if he saw my footmarks in the frost he'd be up to me. I laid down in the ditch, about ten yards from the farthest trap, and about the time as I expected I saw him come up the hedge-side. The first trap had not gone off, but when he came to the other one he made sure as it had had something in it, for it was let off, and drawed out as far as the chain 'ud allow. He picked it up and looked very careful at it, and pulled some ' dawn ' out of the teeth. He tried to make out whether it had come out of a hare or a rabbit; and he first of all shined it up to the light, and then laid it on his hand, and at last he began to set the trap again. He looked all about him very careful, and once he stopped and laid down flat under the hedge, as there was some one coming along the road. It was light enough now to see to the road easy, and I just peeped up, and it was a stranger as had frightened him a bit. When he saw as it was no harm, he got up again and went on to finish the setting. This time he'd got his back towards me, so I crept out as quick as could be, and got close up to him, and give a bit of a cough. He turned round, and I thought he'd have dropped. I says, ' Well, Joe, you've kept me starving a long while waiting of you this morning.' ' Oh, dear,' he says, ' I wish I hadn't kept you at all, Mr. Thornton. I hope you won't say ought about it to the master ; it's the first traps as I ever set, and I've caught nought.' ' No,' I says, ' but that wasn't for want of trying ; let's see what you've had in the trap.' There was some hare dawn, and I showed it him. ' This'll be a bad job for you, Joe ; but get up '—he was kneeled down, just as I'd caught him, all this time—' and come down to the master's.' He was all of a tremble, and I made him go and pick up the other trap, and then we came straight here, sir. Now, he isn't an old hand at it, and the traps never could have caught anything, for they weren't let into the ground, and he'd covered 'em with coarse leaves and grass ; and if you think well, sir, to blow him up and frighten him a bit, I think it'll be enough."

" Well," I said, " let's have him in." Thornton went out of the room, and in about a minute returned with his prisoner.

" So, Ferrier," I remarked, " you've made a sad mess of it this time ; it seems you can't let my hares alone. What have you got to say for yourself, eh ? "

Poor Ferrier looked terribly disconcerted, and made no answer.

" Where did you get those traps from ? " I asked ; " and have you any more of them ? "

" Why, I got 'em, sir, at Amcoats," he replied. " One day, when I went for a load of bones, I was coming out of the town and a man stopped me and says, ' Do you live at Moorside, or thereabouts ? ' ' Yes,' I says. ' Well,' says he, ' then I've got a couple of steel traps, and they're no use to me, as I'm leaving these parts ; but if you like to give me a couple of quarts you may have 'em, and any

of the keepers about your place will give you more than that for
'em.' I give him a shillin', and meant for to sell 'em again; but,
unluckily, I thought I'd just see if they'd catch ought first ! "

" When did you buy them ? " I asked.

" At Amcoats fair, it was, as I met the man."

" What sort of a looking man was he ? "

" Oh, I never seed him afore; but he'd got a ' bran ' face, and a
' O ' like marked on one side "—Thornton and I exchanged glances
—" and he said he ought to be many a mile away afore night."

" Well now, look here, Ferrier," I said; " I happen to know
something about you from Thornton, and he tells me you have never
followed poaching, from what he can make out. I believe your
story about the traps, because I know the man you speak of; and it
was on that very day he sold you the traps that George Oakes
caught him setting hangs on Hayes's farm. I shall keep the traps;
but if you'll promise me not to set any more, and to mind your work
in future, I'll say nothing more about it this once, and I'll tell my
servants not to say you were brought here by my keeper; and, if you
get back to work in good time, your master may never know anything
at all about it." Poor Joe was most intensely happy at getting
off so easily, and I felt satisfied I had done the judicious thing.

When he was gone I asked Thornton if I was quite right in letting
him off, as *a hare had undoubtedly been caught in one of the traps,*
and got out again.

" Why, sir," said he, " I am sure he would not have caught a
hare in a month as them traps was set, and there was no doubt all
the same about some hare-dawn being in one of 'em; but it doesn't
follow, you know, sir, that a hare had been in."

I pressed Mr. Thornton no farther.

It would be about a week after this occurrence that we were
alarmed by seeing a very considerable smoke in the direction of the
moor. I was pruning some rose trees in front of the house, and had
sent Thornton and Oakes (who had been their rounds and had just
come in) for a long ladder, when I fancied I smelt burning weeds or
heath; and, looking round, I distinctly saw a large volume of smoke

in the direction of the moor and the two men coming back to me in a great hurry and without the ladder, they having smelt the smoke and then seen it, just as I did.

Without wasting time in conjecture as to who should have done this piece of mischief, we laid hands on a billhook and a couple of spades, and ran as hard as we could to the moor.

On arriving at the scene of damage, we found a man stripped to his shirt, trowsers, and boots, and thrashing away at the fire with a shovel. Who should it be but my friend, Mr. Joseph Ferrier!

We had no time for more than a few hurried words. Ferrier seeing that we had a billhook, called out as soon as he had ascertained the fact, "I say, George, cut down to the plantin', and bring a rattling good bough or two!" No sooner said than done, and in about a quarter of an hour Oakes returned, and, having now obtained a good weapon each, we laid into the fire with a will, and in half an hour had fairly got it under.

Having done this, it was now time to hear any account Ferrier could give of its commencement, and the following particulars were given us. I shall make the affair more readable by putting it in Ferrier's own words.

"It were a bit sin' as I was setten getting my dinner down at the gravel pit, when who should come up but Dick Scourfield and McDonough. They clapped theirselves down on the grass, and, after a bit, Dick pulls out his pipe and begins to smoke. He'd lighted with a flint and steel, and some 'touch' as he'd used falled down into a patch of heath about as big as my hand like. I suppose it kep on burning, for all of a sudden a little wind set it blazing, and in about two minutes or so it were all burnt. While it were burning, Dick says to his mate, 'Dos't see, lad?' and he says, 'Yar.' I says, 'It's getting very green to burn, isn't it?' Dick says, 'Yar, I should ha' thought so.'

"In about ten minutes they took theirselves off, and I didn't give it another thought; but about an hour and a half ago they both comes to me again, at the quarry, and McDonough says to me, 'Joe,' says he, 'was them two chaps George and Thornton as was here a bit sin' ?' ' I seed no chaps,' says I. ' Yar,' says he, ' but they was past here safe enough.' ' Well,' says I, ' if they was, I didn't see ought on 'em.' With that they turned off and went down the lane. Now, somehow, I guessed as they was after their games, and when they'd got over the brow I went after 'em. They kep on and on till they was nearly got to the next brow, and I was just going back to • my work, when I saw 'em go to the moor wall and climb half up, and then lean over, and one of 'em occasionally pointed with his hand towards the moor. They both got down into the lane together and stooped, and in about a minute or so I could see a little smoke rise up just where they was. One of 'em, I could see, was fanning with his hat, and the smoke got bigger and bigger, and at last it went out. I saw 'em do the same thing again, a yard or two on, but close to the wall ; and, while Dick was stooped down, McDonough was leaned over the wall. I saw the smoke again, and then I guessed they were for firing the moor. I cut off as hard as ever I could for the shovel, and it was a matter of half a dozen minutes before I got back to the top of the hill again, and then, sure enough, I saw four or five bits of fire, and them two rascals setting alight to the moor in different spots. I runned—good Lord how I runned ! to get near 'em. They was some time afore they seed me, and then off they bolted. I knowed the only thing for it was to try and beat it out. If I'd come down to the house, sir, the whole moor 'ud have been burnt before I could find you, perhaps ; and I made sure as you would some on you see the smoke and come to it."

I need not say that Joe was a richer man than before by a couple of sovereigns, and he gained also great applause from the two keepers, and Thornton told him that ninety-nine men out of a hundred would have run off for assistance, and left the mischief to be done during their absence.

Fortunately, the heath was comparatively green, or we should have had the whole moor burnt, without doubt ; and it was just getting the proper time for the grouse to begin to lay.

We went to look at the spot where the heath was first burnt, and we found the two scoundrels had lighted it in the road, and tried to

I

get it to burn through the wall, but had failed; and, finding this to
be the case, had, during Ferrier's absence to fetch the shovel, jumped
over and deliberately fired it on the moor itself, as observed by Joe
on his return.

There had not been wind sufficient to raise a very great flame, or
Joe's hair and whiskers would probably have suffered. As it was,
the poor fellow was nearly choked with the smoke and his great
exertions. I told him to get his waistcoat, necktie, and hat, and
come to the house, and I would give him something to drink. He
hunted about for these articles of attire, but could not find them;
and then it occurred suddenly to him that he had forgotten to note
the exact spot where he had thrown them in his hurry. We all
looked well about, and at last Oakes came across half a dozen brass
buttons, a steel tobacco-box bearing a very pretty shade of blue upon
it, and also the steel-work and blade of a large-sized pocket-knife.
" Oh dear, oh dear ! " said poor Joe; " them's them, and they're all
burnt." " Well, Joe," I replied, " come down home, and I'll find
you something as good as those you've lost; for you've done us a
capital good turn to-day." " Yes, sir," said he, " and I will again ; "
and then he asked me, in a whisper, whether " George had been told
of his having been catched." I assured him he had not by *myself*,
and I could answer for *Thornton*, whereupon Mr. Ferrier looked
decidedly happy.

Arrived at the house, I soon hunted out an old waistcoat and a
hat, and also replaced the necktie with four very good ones for
which I had no further use; and, although I did not say anything at
the time about the loss of poor Joe's knife, I did not forget, on my
first visit to the town, to buy him one that made his eyes glisten
with delight when he saw it.

Altogether I had, by a judicious leniency—to which, however, I
had been instigated by our friend Thornton (who knew all about
Joe Ferrier, very fortunately)—succeeded in making a very staunch
ally. Joe had an honest broad face, and there was not the least
appearance of that " down " look about him which a regular poacher
usually possesses. His first essay in poaching had shown him to

know nothing about it, and I saw, from the way he told his story about the trap, that every word was true.

It was on the 13th of April that he had seen the men set the moor on fire, and this being three days after the time allowed even for legitimate burning, went still more against them when brought up, as they were, before the magistrate, and convicted in the full penalty of 5*l*., and—as Joe told me, triumphantly, on his return home the day that the case had been tried—"cosses."

CHAPTER XVIII.

Dog chopping Doe Hare—Small Leverets—Failure to rear—Trout spearing—
Catching George Woodhall—Penalty—Accidental Death of Flack the
Poacher.

A FEW days after the conviction of Scourfield and M'Donough I
met one of my tenants with a dead hare in his hand. He stated
that it had been killed by one of his dogs, and that he had been
present when it occurred. The dog had pounced on the hare and
mortally injured her before the man could prevent it. There was
no "form" just at the spot, he told me, as far as he was able to
judge from a cursory observation; and he said he was puzzled to
know how it was the hare should have allowed herself to be taken
unawares as one might say. I directed the man to accompany me
to Thornton's cottage, and we should hear what explanation *he*
could give of it. Thornton was not at home, and we had to wait an
hour, but at the expiration of that time he came in and we showed
him the hare. A very short inspection convinced him that she was
suckling young ones, and the reason was now apparent why the
poor creature had been so easily "chopped."

By Thornton's request I at once accompanied him, under the
guidance of the farmer, to the spot where she was first seen, and
after a search among the tussocks we discovered two very small
leverets, which after some difficulty we secured.

"What do you think of them, Thornton?" I asked. Thornton
shook his head. "I doubt, sir, they're too young," he replied.
"I've found such like many a time, and have done all as I knowed
to rear 'em, but it's a great toss-up when they're such little 'uns as
them. If they've ever learnt to nibble a bit of grass they'll do, but
if they're sucking yet it is very little good." "Well," I said, "take
them home, and try what you can do."

I asked every day how they were getting on, and learnt that they took the scalded milk that was given them, and seemed to thrive very well indeed ; and yet Thornton, with all these very favourable circumstances, constantly expressed his fears that they would do no good. In about a week one of the little hares began to look dull about the eyes, and remained jammed in a corner of the box in which they were kept, and when temporarily removed it always went back again to the same spot. In addition to this it began to "scour" and lose weight. Thornton tried new warm milk, but it did no good, and then he tried a slight addition of alum water to the milk, and also a little soda. It was all of no use, however, for at the end of the second day the poor thing died. We still had the other to look after, and it seemed to be doing well ; but the day but one after the death of the first it also began exactly in the same way, and in spite of all that Thornton could do it died. He told me how very difficult it is to bring very young hares up, and that these two had gone off like all previous ones he had known (with few exceptions) and attempted to rear. The scouring when it once sets in cannot be stopped, and is invariably fatal.

I should mention that the man who owned the dog came and begged I would do just as I liked about having it destroyed ; but I made inquiries and found that it had really been done on the impulse of the moment, and that the dog did not make a practice of running hares, so we let him escape.

I believe I have mentioned that among other desirable appendages to my estate there was a small stream of water and a number of ponds. It was with great satisfaction that I discovered two water-hens' nests in a small patch of alder-stumps on the edge of one of the ponds, and I used frequently to go and see whether the young birds had hatched. On one of my visits I happened to observe a slight stir in the water, and going to the spot I found a trout of about half a pound weight, seemingly disabled through some injury. I took it out, and found it marked on the shoulder as if it had been bitten by a pike or an otter. I did not know that there were any of the former in the water, and as to otters I had never before heard of any in so small a stream.

I knocked the trout on the head and put it in my pocket to show to the keeper. On his coming down to the house that evening for any directions I might have to give him, I displayed my capture, and half a minute's examination enabled him to pronounce with an air of authority that the trout had been " speared," and, what was more, it had been done the night before.

Arrangements of course were at once made for watching the stream, and Oakes was instructed to be in readiness after dark. Thornton expressed surprise at spearing being carried on at the ponds, because there was a great deal of mud all round the edges, and the stream running through them was not thicker during the summer than one's arm. I stated my determination to be there myself and assist in the capture of the poachers, and received from my keeper a hint to be careful that the man, if caught, did not mark me in the face with his spear.

About eight o'clock we sallied forth and concealed ourselves behind a hedge running down to the pond where I had found the trout. It was a fine night, but very dark ; and, as no one appeared after two hours' waiting, we began to think our errand would be a useless one for that night, when all at once we observed a light on the pond below us. This was about a hundred yards off, and on the contrary side of the hedge to the one we were on ; consequently, we had to remain perfectly still. The light came nearer and nearer, and at length the bearer of it approached our hiding-place. He had a box strapped round his waist, and a candle burning in the box, which threw its light directly on the water beneath, leaving all surrounding objects apparently darker than before. The man entered the water about half way along the pond-side, and after the lapse of about a minute struck at a fish, but missed it. A second stab was more successful, and he transferred the fish to his pocket. Another followed, and then another, and by this time he seemed to have done all he could at that spot, and came out on to dry land, but entered the water again close to the hedge. He was now within three yards of us, and having struck at and caught a trout, he was putting it away, when Oakes, who had on a pair of Fagg's wading boots, jumped into the water and seized him by the collar with his left hand, and by the arm in which he had the spear with the right. After a bit of a struggle, and a good deal of violent exclamation on the part of the poacher, Oakes dragged him out, and then we saw that it was George Woodhall, whom we had taken previously for rabbit poaching. He had killed eleven trout, and had tried five ponds before he came to the one where we caught him. I examined the spear with considerable curiosity. It was a double blade, formed like a two-pronged kitchen fork, and about the same size, with the exception of the points being about a quarter of an inch wide. It had no barbs, and consequently had to be used with great dexterity to allow of the fish being seized with the left hand before slipping off the spear into the water again. The box was whitewashed inside for the purpose of reflecting a strong light.

Ponds (and especially small ones with a slight stream running through them like mine) are not generally very good places for spearing trout in, as the mud caused by the man in walking—even if ever so slowly—obscures the water and renders the fish difficult to be seen. Spearing is carried out most successfully in small rivers, where the water is very clear ; and an expert poacher in such a locality will take an inconceivable quantity in a short space of time. A 5l. penalty attaches to this offence ; and I was very glad that the magistrate before whom we summoned Woodhall convicted him in the full amount.

Shortly after the event above, there was a great excitement caused in the neighbourhood by the very mysterious disappearance of the eldest son of one of my smaller tenants. He had gone out one morning without leaving word as to the probable direction in which he should proceed ; and a very extensive search, carried out by all the available strength of the neighbouring cottages and farms, was attended with no favourable results. Thornton and Oakes had an idea that the young fellow kept a ferret, but with all their combined ingenuity they could not discover where it was.

Three days had passed over since the man had been first missed, and still no tidings could be discovered of his whereabouts. On the morning of the fourth day one of the labourers having occasion to take a short cut across the moor, arrived at a part where a breast-wall had been built to keep the bank from slipping on to a tramway which was but seldom used. He could perceive that the wall seemed a good deal pulled down, and went to examine the spot. A large heap of stones lay altogether, and the whole of the wall itself, out of which these stones had been pulled, had sunk down about three feet. To the intense surprise and horror of the man he perceived the soles of a pair of strong boots apparently built into the wall. A moment's reflection convinced him that some one was buried underneath, and he at once proceeded to get the stones away as carefully as he could. Half an hour's work disclosed the body of the unfortunate man who had been so long missing. He was still alive, although a great weight of stone had fallen on his back and pressed his chest into the ground. Having dragged him out, he left him on the ground and ran home for assistance. On returning with half a dozen men a ferret was found running about, and the story was now too evident—viz., that Flack (this was the name of the poor fellow) had had the ferret fast and tried to rid him out, and in so doing had let the wall down on himself. Two more days closed the scene, and the unfortunate victim to poaching died at the end of that time, never having recovered consciousness.

CHAPTER XIX.

Thornton makes a "Live-trap"—Description—Rabbit Burrows—Bolt-hole—
Hedgehogs—Netting Hares at Serley's Gates, and turning out again.

I HAD frequently heard Thornton express himself strongly in
favour of a live trap he had invented, but had thought no more
about it until one day when I happened to meet him coming
down the steps from his workshop with a long narrow box under
his arm.

"What have you got there, Thornton?—is it a trap?" I inquired.

"Yes, sir," he answered; "I've just finished it, and was bringing
it into the house for you to look at."

"Well," I said, "let's look at it now." Thornton put the trap
down on the ground. I proceed to describe it as being made of deal,
and two feet four inches long, five inches and a half outside depth,
and three inches and a half in outside width. In the centre of the
top was a lid about a foot long, and, on opening the trap, I saw that
it was divided equally across the centre by a division, in which
division was a small hole. On each side, or, as I should express it,
in each compartment, was a treadle playing loosely on the floor, and
fixed in the treadle was an upright wire arm. Another piece of
wire went from the upright in a horizontal direction, and passed
through a small staple in the roof of the compartment. At each
outer end of the box was a falling door, working very loosely on
two pins. The door being raised with one hand, the horizontal
wire was slipped under the end and propped it up. Any weasel or
stoat running into the trap and pressing, as it would of course do,
on the treadle, must cause it to tilt a little, and the wire being consequently withdrawn the door falls down, and, closing from within,
renders the escape of the vermin utterly out of the question.

I expressed an intention of accompanying Thornton to see how he

set this trap ; and having obtained a spade, which he told me would
be a necessary article in setting it, we started off.

We took the direction of the rabbit warren, and having arrived
there the keeper selected a part where the wall passed over a bank
of no great elevation.   Here he proceeded to dig a trench about a
foot wide and three yards long, and having finished it, he placed the
trap equidistantly from each end, and then made a rough sort of
drain (if one may so call it) from the trap to these points.   There
was a good deal of stone about, so he had no difficulty in forming it,
although he said a " turf " drain could be made with equal facility.
When completed, it certainly presented every appearance of a
common field sough.   Having set the trap, Thornton placed a
stone on the lid and we left it.

He had been tolerably successful with the small running vermin,
but he was short of baits, and was anxious to have as many of the
traps requiring no bait as he could procure.   The weasels and stoats
had certainly begun to invade our territory now that the game was
thicker on the ground, although we had not as yet seen many
leverets besides the two poor unfortunates that Thornton had tried
unsuccessfully to rear ; but we had a good lot of young rabbits,
although there were none large enough to kill as yet.

Coming away from the warren and across one or two of the best
used of the burrows, I made the remark (pointing at the same time
to the object causing it), " What a little bit of a hole a rabbit makes,
Thornton."

" By George, sir," said he, " I hadn't seen that.   We 're not a bit
too soon with that trap, and I must get a lot more down as soon as
I can."

" Why, what 's the particular hurry ? " I asked.

" Because, sir, if you notice that hole's ' blown out,' and before it
was in that form I'll be bound you could not have seen anything.
Rabbits very often work up towards the top of the ground till there 's
only just about the thickness of the roots of the grass between them
and the ' day.'   Now, if any stoat or weasel gets in and pushes 'em
a bit hard they just give a cram against the grass and their heads

are through directly, and where their heads pass they 're not long in forcing their bodies. It isn't a trifle as 'll make 'em blow the hole out, because it shows the spot ; and in fact if you was to dig ever so much they 'd not escape that way, and if a dog scratched at the hole they 'd sit at the far end and know they were safe ; but only turn a ferret in and out they go. No one has been ferreting here I 'm sure, sir, for at this time of the year the poachers aren't so fond of getting a ferret fast among a lot of very young rabbits, for he may stick there for a whole day. No, no, there 's a stoat or a weasel about ; and I dare say I shan't be long before I get him."

About a week had passed and the new trap had been regularly looked at each morning by either Thornton or myself, for I was really most anxious to see whether it would catch. Nothing had as yet been found in it, when one morning, on going to look, and gently raising the lid, the brown back of a stoat was discovered. A very careful investigation showed us that we might proceed to open it wide, for the stoat was quite dead.

"A very odd thing it is, sir," said Henry, "and I never can account for it ; but although I 've caught dozens on dozens of weasels and stoats in these traps, yet I never found one of 'em alive, and what it is as kills 'em passes my comprehension." It certainly was very strange. We had looked at this trap the day before ; and the stoat was in first-rate condition, and had not a mark upon him anywhere. It would appear an anomaly to call it a "live trap" where the inmate is invariably taken out *dead* after, at the utmost, only twenty-four hours' confinement ; but certainly there was nothing about the trap to kill him. We were content to receive the fact as we found it.

We went on to look at some more traps, both steel and wood, but found nothing in them except a hedgehog, which Thornton was about to destroy, when I requested him to let it live, as I did not think they did any harm. "Indeed you 're mistaken, sir," said my keeper ; "they kill any young game they come across, and I know when I was keepering near Bishop Auckland I once turned a hedgehog into a large wire pen with two ducks, and in the morning the ducks were killed, and the head and neck of both of 'em nearly all eaten."

"Well, but," I said, "how do you account for never catching them at fresh-baited traps, for I've heard you say you seldom or never did ? "

"Why, it must be, sir, because they eat beetles and maggots, and such like things 'among-hand,' but I know they *do* kill young rabbits and leverets if they get the chance."

I did not argue the matter any further, but I would not consent to the hedgehog being killed, and, even after hearing Thornton's opinion of their habits, I gave him general directions never to kill them unless so badly hurt as to be evidently incurable. Thornton promised to obey me ; but I sadly fear my wishes would avail a poor hedghog but little should he capture one and I not be present.

The one we had just found had been caught by a fore-leg and part of the shoulder, and it was this latter circumstance that saved the leg from being fractured. I told Henry to put the hedgehog on the ground on the other side of the wall and then come away. We waited for at least a quarter of an hour, and then we saw a slight movement in the great prickly creature ; but this was only caused by his putting his head cautiously out to see that the coast was all clear. He remained perfectly still for many minutes longer, and at last ventured on a short stretch of about a foot ; it ended in his walking, or rather running, off, and I was delighted to see the poor old fellow seemed sound enough.

I have before mentioned that my keeper and myself succeeded in getting on very good terms with Mr. Serley, the freeholder to whom I have alluded ; but as he was a queer sort of a fellow, and not altogether the man to ask favours from, I did not venture to suggest to him the propriety of our putting extra lower bars to his gates, the same as we had done to mine.

Thornton had asked him once if he was not afraid of his lambs getting out and straying away, and had in several other ways tried to "lead up to him," but all was of no use, and, to increase our anxiety, we found that, from the fact of old Serley "boning" his

land and forcing the grass, our hares began to be very fond of feeding there. Although the time of the year was not one usually
selected by the poacher for netting hares, as they would be in effect
"killing the goose for the sake of the golden eggs," yet the practice
was carried on, and we much feared we should lose some doe hares
at this very awkward spot.

Thornton dared not net the hares at this time of the year (May)
as he would in October and later, for in the process of shaking and
frightening them they might get irretrievably injured—I mean, of
course, the doe hares.

He asked me whether I had any objection to his netting the
different gates on this inlying freehold and turning the hares out
again. I told him I could not give any consent in the matter, but
would not control him either one way or the other. Acting upon
this intimation, he at once proceeded to make a light net with
meshes about an inch in diameter. To each end of the string running along the top of the net he fastened an old powder canister
with half a charge of very strong shot in each. The first night of
using the net he ran five hares into it. The meshes being small not
one of the hares was detained more than half a minute, as they could
not get entangled, and the powder canister having been placed on
the gatepost, was pulled violently down directly the net was struck
away, and made a noise in falling to the ground quite sufficient
to frighten the hares most desperately. Thornton did not once
show himself during the operation, and by the end of a fortnight he
had driven as many as fourteen hares.

He then stopped the proceeding, but tried again about the beginning of June. He had several sets, but only caught one leveret
about as large as a full-grown rabbit. This want of success was not,
however, owing to the absence of hares from the feeding ground,
because on each occasion "Bob" had some famous runs, but *the
hares would not look at the gate,* and invariably topped the wall.

CHAPTER XX.

A Day's Magpie shooting in Nesting-time—Habit of Magpie at this Period—
Carrion-Crows also—Hares at "Black Inclosure"—Rabbit driving Hare
away—I catch a Hare in a Steel Trap by Accident.

ABOUT the beginning of June a man came and called upon me to
say that, hearing I was a great advocate for destroying carrion-
crows and magpies, he would be very glad if I would come over or
send Thornton to their place, as they had about a dozen acres of
larch plantation, and not being preserved anywhere round it, the
magpies had made it a breeding-place for years, and they lost their
hen-eggs by scores. The locality was about four miles off, but, as
the pursuit of magpies was rather a favourite diversion with me, I
not only said I would come myself but would bring Thornton also.
Taking a boy with us to stand by the horse, and a rug to throw over
him, off we started the next day. The man met us at the plantation (which we found was nearer twenty acres than twelve), and
we all three proceeded to search for nests. The old birds must be
sitting deep, we knew, or some of them must, in fact, have hatched.
A nest was soon found, and I was whispering directions to the man
as to hitting the tree with a stick, when there was a slight rustle at
the nest, and off the old bird started. Bang ! and down she came
brushing through the trees.

"A smart shot that of yours, Thornton."

"Middling, sir," said Mr. T., with a complacent smile of conscious
skill on his countenance however.

"Shall we pull out the nest ?" I asked.

"Not worth while, sir, so far from home," was Thornton's
reply.

Within a hundred yards we came to another nest, and I was
expecting the same process. The man hit the tree.

"Not on," I said.

"Wait a bit, sir," replied the keeper.

The man struck the tree again, but nothing stirred.

"Can you swarm?" I asked, "because one would like to see if there are eggs or young ones in the nest."

"Not much to reckon on, sir," he replied ; "I used to could at one time, but I get stiff like."

A thought occurred to me that I should send for the lad who was taking care of the horse ; so the man went for him, and took the precaution to bring the horse and cart inside the plantation, and secure him to one of the trees. The boy seemed much elated at the prospect afforded him of showing his skill in swarming, and in a very few minutes he was half-way up to the nest. I had put down my gun, making sure that no magpie that ever existed could stand the noise of small branches snapping off beneath her, to say nothing of the shaking of the tree caused by the exertions of the young gentleman alluded to.

"You had better be ready, sir," said Thornton. "I've seen 'em let you get right up to the nest before they'd start."

"Well, I'm sure she's not there now," I answered.

The lad had by this time got nearly to his destination, and in fact was investigating the nest with a view to find the aperture through which the old magpie entered, when he suddenly exclaimed, "Here her is! Mind *me* !"

I could hardly credit it, but out she most certainly did burst. Bang! and a muttered exclamation from Mr. Thornton, followed instantly by bang! again.

"I missed her that time, I doubt, sir," said Henry; "but it was about as awkward a spot to shoot as one could well have. I saw her appear at the hole as she went off; but I daren't shoot for fear of hitting Michael. I fancied, too; I was fair on with the second barrel, though I know I shot a bit behind her with the first. It's a mess ; but it can't be helped."

The boy meanwhile had descended the tree, and was busy brushing off the bits of lichen and moss from his clothes.

"Hark! what a queer noise," I remarked. It resembled the sound cr-r-r-r-r, repeated at a few moments' interval.

Thornton went on a few. yards in the direction whence the noise came.

"All right, sir! She's here. I couldn't help fancying it was a bit strange if I missed her clean."

So far we had done pretty well; but the magpies having had a very long and uninterrupted reign, it was no very difficult matter to find another nest.

The one we had just disposed of contained six eggs, and they were close on the point of hatching, which fully accounted for the old bird being so unwilling to go off. I could not have believed any bird would sit so deep had I not seen what I did; but Thornton said it was a very common occurrence, especially with magpies. Carrion-crows, though they may allow the tree to be struck several times consecutively, and even stones to be thrown at the nest, will not stand a person offering to swarm the tree without leaving it. Thornton suggested (and I thought with a good deal of reason) that a carrion-crow sitting on an open nest is conscious that she may be seen; but that, as long as her tree is not actually climbed, the enemy may have a doubt about it. The latter operation at once convinces her that she has probably been perceived, and then away she flies. Now a magpie is utterly invisible from below when sitting, and she takes care she shall continue so as long as there is a chance.

On blowing aside the feathers on the breast of the last magpie, a bare place, as large as half the palm of one's hand, was visible, and it was quite white and puckered, as if there was a deposit of water just under the skin. The feathers must have been worn off by the long-continued operation of sitting, for no feathers are ever used in the lining of a magpie's nest. The dry fibrous roots of grasses are invariably employed.

I have mentioned the fact that we had very soon discovered another nest, and I had been warned by my keeper that I might expect at any time a very opposite line of conduct on the part of an old magpie to what had just been displayed; consequently we approached the nest next discovered with our guns all ready.

"Yon's it, sir," whispered the man, pointing to a very full-blown specimen of a nest. The words were hardly uttered when there was a rustle, followed by the instant appearance of the old magpie. My gun was thrown up to the shoulder and the trigger pulled all in one movement, and, to my very intense satisfaction, the magpie fell knocked all to "smithereens!" I could not help rushing forward to pick up the bird, but you may judge of my disappointment when I saw Thornton coolly loading again.

"Why, surely you did not shoot?" I exclaimed.

"Yes I did, sir," said Thornton, "but I don't think there was much occasion, for you'd have nailed her dead enough without me. Of course I know better than to shoot at the same time as a gentleman when it's *game*, but with them things it doesn't do to miss any chances."

"Of course not," I said; "and that old magpie caught it sharply between us."

When I came to reflect, however, I could not stifle the accusation of my own conscience, which told me, as plain as it could speak, that I was not "fair on" to a yard when I pulled the trigger; and if it was *my* shot that killed the magpie it must have been a desperate "fluke," and the gun must have spread more than I had ever previously given it credit for.

Thornton, of course, as in duty bound, persisted in saying it was all my doing, and in the presence of the farmer and the boy I did not gainsay it.

We followed up our diversion with very considerable success, and out of thirteen nests we accounted for nine old birds, of which number I did certainly kill three in very good style. Two nests had young ones in, which we threw down, and two old magpies were missed, though I am happy to say not *by myself*, as I did not shoot in either instance, and really they were almost impossible shots for anyone to hit.

Altogether I passed a most agreeable day, and was quite sorry

K

when it was ended and we had to return home. Having arrived at the " Black Inclosure " I told the boy to drive the cart home, and Thornton and myself would take a walk round to see if any hares were out feeding. In one of the fields was a brace of hares very near to the wall, and we sat down to watch if any more would come out. In about a quarter of an hour a rabbit made his appearance, and after inspecting the two hares for a short time he made a dash at the nearest one to him, and pursued it fairly for at least fifty yards, when it escaped into the wood. He took no notice of the other hare, but began feeding on his own account. Thornton much wanted to get a shot at him, but the instant he stirred the rabbit withdrew from the scene.

Thornton remarked that it was very provoking that the rabbits should have spread so far as this plantation, for it was our best hare ground, and they could never agree together. He knew of an old rabbit burrow about a couple of hundred yards in, and we went to see if it was used. There was undoubtedly some fresh scratching about it, and the burrow itself seemed padded. I made a mental resolve that I would be beforehand with Thornton and catch this rabbit, but did not tell him as much.

That very same evening I returned to the spot with a steel trap, which I set at the burrow and covered it carefully over with sand. I had previously sent Thornton in a totally different direction, so that I might have the whole affair strictly to myself.

The next morning off I started to look at the trap, and what was my surprise when I found it was gone! I searched about, and at last I detected a movement among the heath about fifty yards off. On going to the spot I was horrified to find a poor hare in the trap, and one of her fore-legs badly broken. I took out my knife, and, after considerable difficulty, secured the hare and cut off the leg, which was held fast by the principal sinew. She went off at a famous pace, but it was a shocking fracture, and I was more annoyed than I could express.

As soon as I met Thornton I told him of this mischance, and he showed no surprise at it, but said that in the spring and early summer months it is very dangerous to set steel traps at rabbit holes unless they are put very far down, for hares, and especially the jacks, are most inquisitive, and will potter about on dry sandy mounds almost as commonly as rabbits do; and if the trap set for rabbits happens to be tolerably clear of the mouth of the burrow, you may catch a hare almost as certainly as if you set in a "run" on purpose.

He said that it was a pity I had not told him of my intention the afternoon previously, as he would have forewarned me of the possible consequences. As to the rabbit, he meant to wait for him with a gun that evening.

CHAPTER XXI.

" Travelling " Poachers—Oakes and Broadley see them at the Town—Sponge in Cart—Ruse of the two Keepers—Description of the Poachers.

THE post one morning brought me a letter from an old friend, containing the offer of a retriever, which he was parting with solely on account of giving up shooting ; and so convinced was my correspondent that the dog would suit me that he went on to say he had consulted the time-table and found the dog would be delivered at our town about half-past eleven; but he cautioned me that it was a savage and uncertain-tempered animal, and that I had better be cautious who I sent for it.

I had determined to undertake the task myself, but, on second thoughts, came to the conclusion that I had better perhaps take some one who was more accustomed to dogs (and especially strange ones); consequently I sent in to Oakes's cottage, and luckily found that he was at home.

Having ordered the horse to be put in the Whitechapel, Oakes started off a short cut across the land, telling me he would join me a mile away on the road. A few minutes' drive discovered my under keeper seated on a gate waiting my arrival. We drove on for a short distance, and suddenly Oakes, who had his eyes always sharply about him, exclaimed, " There's Henry, sir, and I think he wants to speak to you." That worthy was observed running towards us along a hedge-side, evidently wishing for an interview.

" Well, Thornton ? "

" Good morning, sir ; I beg pardon for stopping you, but are you going to Amcoats ? "

" Yes," I replied.

" Then, if you see any of the keepers, will you please tell 'em that I've just met Morewood, and he says that there's two men stopping somewhere about these parts as drives out almost every day in a spring cart. They've got a gun, and a sort of retrieving snap with 'em, and they're nailing the hares by odd 'uns all up and down. Old hares and leverets seems all alike to 'em. Morewood says he's known of 'em a goodish bit, and hasn't told the neighbouring keepers because he wanted to catch the two rascals himself, but he can't manage it. He saw 'em fire a shot last evening, and no doubt, he says, they 'gathered,' for they both stood up in the cart after the gun went off, and drove at a foot's pace, looking towards the same spot, and in about a minute they both stooped down, and then started off a good rattle. Of course, sir, they'd taken the hare from the dog, and put 'em both under the seat. Morewood was on the brow of a hill at the time, and couldn't see the dog, but he's sure this was how they did it, for when he caught sight of 'em a mile on they'd no dog running with the cart. It 'ud be as well, sir, just to 'incense' any of the keepers that you may see ; and as it's market day, there's like enough to be some of 'em about in the town."

On arriving at Amcoats we put up the horse, and learnt from the omnibus driver that a dog had been sent for me. We went down to the station to bring him away, and on my return I was saluted by a touch of the hat from a fine-looking fellow, standing at the entrance to the inn yard. I returned the salute, and, seeing that Oakes and the stranger were known to each other, I asked him who it was, and he told me it was Broadley, keeper to Colonel Chambers.

"I'll tell him, then," I said, "about these two poachers in the spring cart."

I beckoned to him, when he came up, and, like a civil fellow, repeated the salute ; "You're Broadley, Colonel Chambers's keeper, ar'n't you ?"

"Yes, sir, I am."

"Well, my keeper, Thornton, has heard from Morewood " (who, I should tell the reader, was head keeper to Sir Henry Mansel) " that two men are staying somewhere, either in Amcoats or one of the towns about, and they regularly drive out on the public roads and shoot hares or anything they can come across, and they've a dog with them.   Have *you* heard anything about it ? as, if you haven't, my man wished you to know."

"No, sir," he replied, "it's all new to me."

"Well," I said, "make any inquiry you can, and if you hear anything let me know, or Thornton, or Oakes ; and if *we* do, we can let *you* know."

I then went into the town, having previously told Oakes to get me a sack of Indian corn and some other things.

By four o'clock I was ready to return home, and went back to the inn, where I found Oakes waiting for me.

"Can I speak to you by yourself somewhere, sir ?" he asked.

"Yes," I replied, "anywhere you like.   Shall we go into the saddle-room ?"

"That'll do, sir ; but, as I've found out something about the two men as shoot the hares, and, for anything I know, they may be looking at us *now*, I'd better bring out a headstall or something, to seem as if I was showing you that the 'harnish' wants mending, and then we can go back into the saddle-room and I'll tell you all about it, sir."

This seemed a praiseworthy step, and within five minutes we might have been observed closely investigating the fastening of the chin-strap of somebody's headstall, but *whose* goodness only knows. The owner would doubtless have been amazed had he happened to come up at the moment, and found two strangers deeply intent on a microscopic examination of what I remember was a very decided specimen of country saddlery, in an advanced stage of decomposition through the abundant use of the most villanous-smelling train oil. To make it worse, it would appear as a double insult by our evidently not considering the light afforded by the window of the saddle-room as sufficient, but subjecting the imperfections above alluded to to the blessed light of heaven at four o'clock on a fine day in May !

About two minutes seemed to suffice for our inspection, and we then withdrew into the room.

"I've got to know something about it, sir," Oakes commenced. " When the Indian corn came into the yard I told the man to set it

down off the sack barrow, and I would cast about for some one to
help me with it into our cart, as he looked but weakish. The ostler
was 'fast' with some one's horse, and I looked out into the street,
when up comes Broadley again, so I asked him to give me a lift, and
we took the sack up between us. *I* happened to be walking backwards, and Broadley mistook another cart for ours. We set the sack
down ; Broadley held up the apron, to see that there was nothing as
could be crushed ; and I was just then brushing a dust of flour off my
arm, and did not see what he was doing till he says,

" ' I say, George, where did that blood come from ?'

" ' What blood ?' I says.

" ' Why, look yer, there's a great dab of blood on the floor of
your cart ; and if it didn't come out of a fresh-killed hare's ear I'm a
Dutchman.'

" Sure enough, sir, there it was, and it hadn't been long there,
neither.

" ' Well, but,' says I to Broadley, ' hold on ! This isn't our cart !'

" ' Don't make a row !' he says all of a sudden, quite gentle-like.
' Here's them two, for a thousand.'

" I guessed what was up, and didn't look round, but very quietly
helped Broadley in with the corn into our own cart, and we walks
out of the yard together.

" I looked out of the corner of my eye and saw the men plain
enough. They were dressed in dirtyish check shooting-coats, and
had on gaiters and breeches ; and I could tell plain enough as they
were looking me and Broadley over middling sharp, but *they'd seen
nothing*.

" We walks out, as I said, sir, and Broadley whispers, ' Come to
the Cheese in five minutes !'

" Nobody could tell as he'd spoken, for he didn't look at me ;
and when we got into the street I went one way and he went
another, and in about five minutes I made off for the Cheese, and
just as I got in sight of it I saw Broadley going in, so I joins him.

" The landlord of the Cheese had been a groom of Sir Henry
Mansel's, and him and Broadley was great friends, sir ; so as soon as

we gets into the house Broadley called the master o' one side, and
told him all about it. Then he asked him to lend him an old great-
coat and a shawl handkercher; and while he looked 'em out for
him Broadley goes into the washus and cuts a bit off a sponge as
was in the soapbox over the slopstone, and then he got the missis to
fry a bit of fat bacon and to give him some black cotton. He ties
the cotton round the sponge, leaving the ends about a couple of
inches long, and then he asked for a small nail, and fastened the
cotton round it just under the head. The landlord lent him a hammer, and he dips the sponge in the bacon-dripping till it was soaked
through, puts on the great coat and the handkercher (which he tied
round his mouth and chin), and, having borrowed the landlord's
hat, off he goes.

"He told me to wait, sir, till he got back, and in half an hour in
he comes again, and I saw he'd made something out."

"'Well, George,' says he, when we'd got into the back bar, 'I've
done it as nice as pie, and, what's more, I've nailed the dog, or I'll
give over guessing. I hobbled into the yard, walking lame-like,
and what should I see but the same two fellers watching the ostler
putting their horse in. I saw I must be sharp about it if I looked
to settling the dog; and I says to the ostler, 'There's a 'nation
great fire, I expect, in the next street; I never seed such a one out of
London.' The two men cut out to have a look, and I says, 'I'll
hold the horse a minute or two, Jem, if you want to be off.' Out
he goes, and as soon as he was in the street I whips out the hammer
and nails the sponge under the seat of their cart inside, and high
up. I'd just got hold of the horse's head again when the men
comes back, and Jem too; and very savage they were, but I said I
supposed it must have been a chimney on fire as I'd mistook, and
at last they thought theirselves as it must have been. They didn't
stay any longer at after, but got into the cart and drove off.'

"'Now, Jem,' says Broadley to the ostler, 'I want to know the
names of them two, and I got 'em out of the yard to look if there
were a name on the back of the cart, but there wasn't.' Jem asked
what for; but Broadley knowed too well to trust him. However,

he couldn't tell him aught, except as they come the market day
afore, and had a hamper with 'em as they took away. No doubt
they sent off a lot of hares in it from the station."

This was what Oakes and Broadley had been able to make out,
and it was very evident that the only plan *now* was to keep a
general and careful watch all along the public roads, and spread the
description of the two men as widely as we could amongst all the
neighbouring keepers.

The dress they appeared in on that day would be very little
clue, as of course they took good care to change it even in the cart
when travelling. Broadley and Oakes described them as follows :
One was a man of about forty years of age, five feet nine high, and
stoutly built ; he had black whiskers cut closely, but covering a
good deal of his face. The other was about the same height, but
very hollow-chested, and with bow legs—a sort of fellow who could
run fast and keep it up well also ; he was a " down-looking " man,
and had a " hare lip "—rather *àpropos*, by the bye, of his vocation
in our neighbourhood.

That these two gentry were " town hands " we had little doubt,
and that their detection would be a matter of great difficulty was
tolerably apparent.

I mentioned my fears of ultimate success to Thornton ; but that
talented individual treated it as a very matter-of-fact affair.

" I can catch 'em, sir, but I should have a better chance if I did
it on some of the other property where they've got more hares than
us, for they'll go where there's most, depend upon it. That dog
will be good for another week, and *then* it's all up with *him ;* and if
we don't catch 'em before then we may give it up, as they won't
stop after *he's* dead. If you don't mind, sir, I'll step over and see
Arden about it all."

CHAPTER XXII.

Thornton consults with Arden—Morewood (Sir Henry Mansel's Keeper) dis-
covers the two Poachers' Abode—His Son acts as " Spy "—The Keepers make
up a " Dummy " Hare—They form an Ambush, and capture the two Poachers.

I DID not see Thornton till the day but one after our last interview,
and when I did come across him he seemed to have but little to
communicate. He had been to consult Arden, and all he would
confide to me was that a plan of capture had been arranged, but
whether it would answer or no was a very different affair.

I was engaged in my dressing-room at about half-past seven in
the morning after this last conversation with my head keeper, when
I overheard the words, evidently in reply to a question asked, " Yes,
in about ten minutes, I should fancy ; I took up the hot water a
good end of half an hour back."

Being in anxious daily expectation of some intelligence from my
keeper, I opened the door and called out to know if I were wanted.
The servant replied that Thornton and Morewood were waiting to
see me.

I need not say I was down stairs in a very few seconds, and the
two keepers followed me, by my direction, into the breakfast-room.

" Ah, I see you've caught them, Thornton," was my remark.

" Oh, yes, sir. They're caught at last, but not on our ground.
Morewood, here, has done 'em upon theirs."

" Well, and tell me all about it," I said.

" Why, sir," replied Morewood, " since I saw Henry fust about
these men shooting, I determined to have one more try after the
spot as they were stopping at, and it struck me as it was not a bit
unlikely as they'd be putting up at some low kind of place a goodish
bit off; so I sent our Ben the same afternoon as far as the Cross
Guns, on the Norton-road, and told him to make out all he could

from the landlord. I knew he wouldn't tell us anything as 'ud help us very much, but there could be no harm in trying. The Cross Guns is better than seven miles away from us, and I don't know as Fox (the landlord) had ever seen Ben.

"He reached the house about half-past four, and found Fox and his wife at tea. He went right in and waited to see if they knew who he was, but he saw in half a minute as it was all right about that, for Fox says, 'Now, young 'un, what do you want?'

"'I want nought but a drop o' beer,' says Ben, and he set hisself down not far from the fire. In about five minutes he hears all of a sudden some man say, 'Get under, yer brute, and lie down!' The voice seemed to come from the back parlour, and then Ben heard some one trying the lock of a gun as plain as could be. He didn't seem to take the least notice, but the landlord jumped up and went to the room door, and said something to the feller inside. Ben couldn't hear what it was, but in a second or so Fox came back, and a man with him. Ben could see as they were 'looking him over,' but he sat staring at the fire as if he knew nought about 'em.

"The man says, 'Have you a drop of sweet oil, Mrs. Fox? for the blade of my pocket-knife works so stark, it will be wearing the spring away.' She hadn't any oil, so the man took a bit of butter off a pat as was on the table, and made no end of a job of putting some on to the spring of the knife.

"'Yes, my lad,' thinks Ben, 'you fancy you have made me safe; but, thank yer, I know the working of a pair of locks a bit too well to be took in in that way.'

"'Well, and which road have yer come?' says Fox, when the man had gone back into the room.

"'Me?' says Ben; 'oh, I came from Boston.'

"'Well, but you have not walked?' says Fox.

"'Oh, no; I come by the railroad as far as Norton.'

"'And what are you for, down here?'

"'Oh, I'd do a bit of farm-work like, and any sort of labouring jobs,' says Ben.

"It was very lucky, sir," said Morewood to myself, "that Ben had lived most of his time with my missis's father at Boston, and in fact, sir, he only come to be at home since the old man died, and that was within nine months. If he'd been living all along with us, Fox 'ud ha' known him.

"He was just going to ask him something more, when the man in the back room calls out, ' I say, Fox!'

" ' Now then!' was the answer.

" ' Come here ; I want to speak to you.'

" Fox goes into the room, and Ben heard a good deal of whispering, and all of a sudden a voice as he hadn't heard before says, ' I'll be hanged if I don't.'

" Ben knew tolerably well *now* that the two men as we wanted were in that very room, and, what was more, they wished to come out and be off, for it was after five o'clock. He paid for the beer as he'd had, and started ; but he waited first of all for Fox to come into the house-place, so as to ask him which was the next town, and how far it was off. Fox came to the door with him as eager as possible, so as to get him out of the way, no doubt."

The sequel I shall give in the substance as it was narrated to me.

Fully determined to see the end of it all, Ben walked briskly away for a few hundred yards, and then got over the hedge and doubled back, so that he could command a good view of the house ; and it was not long before Fox came out, accompanied by the man who had had the knife, and another. They all went into the yard, and presently Ben heard the noise of wheels, and then Fox appeared leading their horse, which was harnessed to a spring cart.

The two men got in, and, after looking round very cautiously in every direction, the landlord went into the house and came out with a brown snap in a chain. He seemed to be looking for the coast to be clear, and then he took the dog up in his arms and put him under the driving seat. Ben did not see any gun, but no doubt one of the strangers had it in his pockets. They drove close past Ben, who was concealed behind the hedge, and that was all he had to tell.

It was a great point, having found out the temporary abode of these two rascals; and that Thornton and Morewood profited by the knowledge was soon to be made evident.

It was tolerably certain that the men would not attempt a shot on any preserved land within reasonable distance of the Cross Guns, so the two keepers set to work to prepare a "dummy" hare for their enemies, and the land on which they decided to try it was some very exposed open ground, with but little apparent cover from whence to watch. This sort of country would better disarm suspicion than one cumbered with thick hedgerows, where the shooters might suspect the presence of a watcher. The only difficulty was to make a sufficient, and at the same time an apparently casual, ambush.

Morewood suggested a large "pot-crate" covered with manure, or at all events with litter of some kind; but Thornton objected that it would appear unlikely to have led out manure in the middle of May, and still more unlikely for a hare to feed within shot of a novel object, for she would require a week to get familiarised with it, and in that week no end of mischief might be done.

At length they decided that one of them should lie at full length in the hedge where it happened to be just thick enough for concealment, and run his chance of a few grains of shot catching him, should he be in a line with the gun and hare when the men shot.

To make a mock hare there was nothing for it but to shoot a live one and stuff it, and this was done the very first thing that evening. The attitude was wonderfully good; she appeared sitting upright, with her ears pricked up, and heels not quite touching the ground; in fact, in the attitude a hare always assumes on taking the first pace into a field from the hedge-side. Inside the shoulder was a piece of very strong leather, a part of an old carthorse collar.

The next morning, at daybreak, Thornton and Morewood proceeded to the spot, and tossed which of them should be in the hedge, and which be watching within easy reach. The toss was won by Thornton, and Morewood proceeded to put on a rough great coat, to guard as much as possible against stray shots. His leggings and breeches were thick enough to resist any reasonably strong shooting gun, and he carried a stone with him to put before his face. The hare was planted about ten yards above him, by the hedge-side, and Thornton hid himself where he could command a view a good way along the road.

An hour had passed, and there were no signs of any spring cart; the only incident that happened during that interval was the conduct of a boy who was coming along the road and caught sight of the hare, and when he had shouted at it for five minutes he commenced throwing stones for another equally extended period, wondering, no doubt, why the hare still remained insensible to his pressing attentions.

Thornton was at last compelled to get up and call to him, and to say that if he wasn't off he would "have him up." This had the effect of putting him to flight, and the keeper had no sooner got hidden again than he saw the long-wished-for cart appear on the brow, about a quarter of a mile off. He had his "binocular" out, and could plainly see that the two men in the cart were looking anxiously on each side of the road as they drove along. They seemed to catch sight of the bait instantly, and they were only going a walking pace at the time. Without stopping the cart, the non-driver had the gun up and fired. The shot striking against the thick leather sewn inside, caused the hare to roll over as naturally as possible, and on the instant their snap dog came bolting out, and made for the hare almost as certainly as if he had seen it shot. Before the dog could get hold of it, Morewood sprang out and took possession of the hare, and the two men catching a hurried view of the turn things were taking, but having their attention undividedly fixed upon the dog and Morewood, gave Mr. Thornton time to emerge from *his* concealment. When they would on the next instant have fled with the precipitation their wiry, half-bred horse entitled them to expect, they found that excellent person in firm possession of the "head" of the quadruped just alluded to.

"Well," said Mr. T. to the man who had shot, "I suppose you've got the other barrel. Hadn't you better try your hand at me or my mate ? "

This little sarcasm wound up the pair to a pitch of the utmost fury, and the " gun-man " swore that if there had been only one of them he'd have settled him.

" Ay ! but there's two on us," said the keeper, " so that might turn out okkard. But come, let's just know your names, and I dare say we can hear you better at the police-office, for somehow I've a notion you won't fancy giving your names too like the real 'uns. Besides, I think I can lead the tit better than you can drive him."

The procession was soon formed, and their final destination was my own house, where they had just arrived, and the whole turn-out was then in the stable-yard, under the watchful eye of a policeman.

Having heard the foregoing account I went out, and was saluted with a volley of abuse from the two prisoners, who at once declined to give any names at all, but swore they would " fetch the law " for myself, Thornton, Morewood, and anyone else they could implicate in their capture.

CHAPTER XXIII.

I purchase Mr. Serley's Property—Description of Plantation—Painting Meuses
—I find some of them stopped—Marking Wall—We wait for the Poachers—
They arrive.

THE estate of my neighbour Mr. Serley—the crabbed old farmer whose small freehold wedged into my property and interfered with its preservation—had often been looked upon by me with an envious eye, and I had repeatedly sounded him on the subject of selling; but he seemed to turn a deaf ear to all inuendoes of the kind, and I had quite given up every hope of becoming the purchaser. I had reason, however, to know that he very much appreciated the service my keepers had once rendered him in discovering the sheep when they were " overdriven " in the deep snow. It was with great satisfaction, therefore, that I heard it rumoured in the neighbourhood that our friend had half a mind to dispose of his property and to give me the refusal.

I had generally made a practice of driving over to our town on market days, where, at the principal hotel, I used to meet my neighbouring landowners; and as we had formed a " County Club " at this same hostelry, we could discuss the general subjects of the day and arrange shooting and other parties.

On one of these market days I was returning home and happened to overtake Mr. Serley, who, as was usual with him, preferred to make the journey on foot. I pulled up and begged he would avail himself of a seat in the dog-cart, which he did with much seeming willingness, and, to my great satisfaction, made me the offer to buy his property. The terms of purchase were settled in a very few minutes, and six weeks from that time saw me installed as owner. The estate, although a small one, possessed very great capabilities for preserving, and amongst other desirable features it presented that of a beautiful square plantation, consisting of 'larch about fifteen years old, with patches of heath and fern growing irregularly all over it, where not shaded by the trees.   Unfortunately, however, sheep had been allowed to run all through it while the trees were much younger, and, where they had not been topped by the sheep, they had been stunted in their growth by these animals rubbing against them and leaving wool sticking to the bark and short branches ; and nothing seems so poisonous to any sort of pine as this—I have, in fact, always found it to be so.   The plantation I allude to covered about fourteen or fifteen acres, and was as nearly square as possible. The walls were in a ruinous condition, and had been built originally full of meuses.   Investigation showed that the setting of these had formed the subject of many and many a poaching excursion.   Scores of them were stopped with a coping, and here and there one left judiciously open.   To render these "safe" seemed an Augean task, and I had arranged with Thornton to get a great quantity of posts and rails to put down inside the wood, in addition to those placed outside, as carried out on other parts of my *original* property.

Thornton had fully come into my views on the matter, and we should soon have commenced the work, when one morning he made a suggestion which appeared to have a good deal of ingenuity in it, and the plan he proposed was as follows—viz., to post and rail, and also wire the land *outside* the wood, but to *paint meuses* on the inner side the wall with some cheap but durable black paint.   No sooner thought of than carried into effect.   I had had the gaps in the walls mended up, and, as the walls themselves were nearly five feet high, I had considered it better to do this than to lower them a foot, which in a very large extent would cost a good deal of money.   We found also on a second inspection that it really would be a difficult matter to set a long net inside, because the trees grew close up to the walls, and there were sufficient patches of heath here and there to prevent such a net being readily got down.   We therefore compiled a mixture of lamp-black, boiling water, and alum, and having reopened all the meuses, we proceeded to paint others between them at intervals of three yards, and put thin pieces of slate, also painted

L

black, in every *real* meuse, to act as a paviour and hide the ground, so that in a moderately dark night the real meuses should not be distinguishable from the sham ones.

Thornton and I both went the same evening, when it was quite dark, to test the effect of that gentleman's ingenious suggestion, and we really found the deception perfect. All we now wanted was practical proof of the success of our plan, but it was many weeks before we were favoured with the coveted result. The adjacent land having been unpreserved during Mr. Serley's *régime*, I suppose the poaching fraternity had not thought it worth their while of late years to trouble it much, as they would have a vast deal of setting to but little purpose. The walls, as I before said, were full of gaps, and hares would, if pursued at night by a dog, prefer these to a meuse, especially if hard pressed. I took care to have the wood well looked to, for I knew perfectly well that when the stock of hares began to increase this would be one of our best covers.

I had now got into the habit of doing a good amount of keepering myself, and, in fact, used to tell my men from time to time, what part of the estate I would devote to my own personal inspection.

It was on one Sunday afternoon that I took a round, intending to come back by the wood—"The Doctor's Plantin'" was the name of it—when I found on arriving there that a meuse was stopped. The next one was the same, and so on for about fifty yards. This rotation was observed all throughout. I could find no stones on the wall, or any "mark," and rather wondered at it. Directly I got home I named the matter to Thornton, and told him to get some men and have it watched. " All right, sir," said that worthy individual, " we 'll wait till they mark the wall, and then we 'll have 'em." " Well, but," I said, " surely they mean to come at once ? " " Oh no, sir, those meuses must remain stopped for a goodish bit— perhaps a week, or it may be a fortnight. The poachers 'll come at daybreak, or perhaps at dinner time, or some time when they think no one's about, and they'll clap a small stone on the wall over every open meuse. We'll have 'em, sir, if we can; but we'll make fools of 'em first.   You'd better let *me* tent that planting till they come."

I willingly gave way to the sagacious Mr. T., and longed for the time when " business " might be reported as imminent.

The week presupposed by my head-keeper had passed, and another after that, and still no sign of an intention to " set." Four days after the expiration of the fortnight Thornton came and told me that the wall was marked, and the invasion of my territory would probably take place that night.   I determined to " head the boarders" myself, and about eight o'clock we sallied out.   The party consisted of myself and my two keepers, and three under-keepers belonging to Colonel Chambers.   Thornton had started an hour before to shift the marks, and by that process to " make fools " of the poachers, as previously suggested.   We found him waiting for us at the corner where I had found the first meuse stopped.   The men had all got " beehive " hats on, and I, not possessing one, was content to fill the crown of my hard wide-awake with moss. Thornton arranged our forces so that he, myself, and Morton (one of the three under-keepers mentioned) should remain where we were, and the others proceed to the opposite corner of the wood in a direct line from where we were posted.

Oakes was furnished with a ball of thin twine, and, leaving one end in Thornton's hand, his party set off to take up their position ; and in case either division heard the approach of the enemy, a slight twitch on the twine (which of course lay close to the ground, and touching the wall, so as not to be kicked by any person advancing to set a purse-net) would be an intimation of the circumstance to those at the other end.

Nine o'clock, ten, eleven, had passed, and no sign of anything. The stillness was oppressive.   I quite longed for a termination to this state of breathless suspense, in which my faculties of hearing were strained to their utmost.   A nightjar began chattering, and, although he was probably a quarter of a mile off, I should have considered he was within six yards.   While listening to the bird and wishing he would " drop it," as it seemed to make the void more disagreeable, one of the men just pressed my ankle gently between his finger and thumb, and I could, on looking slowly round to my right, see four men standing by the wall on the same side as ourselves. In about half a minute they stooped, and, following one another in a most ghostlike fashion under the trees, crossed the corner of the plantation, emerging at the wall side where our twine-signal lay. Thornton had, as soon as he perceived them, given it a twitch; and this was returned to him twice, to show it was received and understood. It had been previously arranged between Oakes and Thornton that one jerk meant "here they are;" two, "get up and come softly this way," and a loud whistle meant "charge!"

I must admit that when I saw we were "in for it," and another five minutes must see us either in desperate combat with a lot of midnight poachers (who perhaps formed only a part of a much larger lot), or in active demonstration of the "pursuing practice," I felt anxious. I was not *afraid*. No; it was more like a desire to be "at work" and get it over without further delay; but a little delay was necessary, or we should spoil everything.

CHAPTER XXIV.

Signal given to charge—We miss the Poachers for a Time—Morton's
impromptu Mode of drawing them—His Capture of one—Nets used—
Result of painting Meuses and shifting Marks—Manners of our Prisoner—
Conviction—Rook Stealer—Conclusion.

ABOUT five minutes were allowed to elapse, and then the precon-
certed signal of two pulls was given, and we ourselves at the same
instant rose very gently up and advanced towards our comrades, of
course having the poachers between us. We had not gone, however,
more than thirty yards before we came upon one of them, who,
having set a net, was crouched down watching it. He sprang to his
feet and gave a loud whistle, and at the same instant rushed into
the wood. Once there, he was comparatively safe, and if his
associates had taken the alarm and followed the same plan, it was
very considerable odds against our making a capture. We met our
own men, but they had caught no one, and in fact the poachers had
one and all concealed themselves. Thornton suggested, in a hurried
way, the only possible means of securing any of them, and the plan
seemed feasible. We were to distribute ourselves round the wood
outside the walls, and, there being six of us, we had rather a better
chance than if we had only numbered four.

Not a moment was lost in running to take up our different posi-
tions, but for a quarter of an hour nothing came of it. Fortunately,
it was a very still night, so that if any of the poachers attempted to
quit their hiding-places and gain the open country, the chances were
they would be heard.

Our proceedings had evidently, as I considered, disturbed the fields
to a certain extent, for the sheep began to make a noise, and one in
particular kept up a tolerably constant bleating. I do not know
how it was that I should be listening intently, as I certainly was to

this sound, because the fact of cattle being disturbed by a loud whistle in the middle of a very quiet night was not so very remarkable. Be this as it may, a very well-executed bleat was suddenly nipped in the bud, and, changed evidently by the "bleater," to a ringing shout of " Help ! "

I need not say that at this cry I ran as fast as I could in the direction of the alarm, and found a fierce battle going on. It appears that Morton had left his waiting-place, run off across one of the fields, and jumped over the wall. From this spot he had proceeded to imitate the bleat of a sheep, and in a few minutes three of the poachers came running to him, and he had seized the biggest of them as he jumped down. The other two, finding their mistake, had attacked Morton with considerable energy, and he, throwing his stick on to the ground, and grasping the poacher he had caught by both sides of his collar, had rapidly opposed his prisoner to the combined attack of his friends. So, taking care to keep his own head low down, he had judiciously subjected that of the poacher to a quick succession of tremendous whacks from their sticks, which, while Morton was shouting for "help" as before stated, induced a vocal accompaniment in an equally energetic roar of "murder!" from his captive.

The two poachers did not forget to keep an eye to windward, and consequently had sufficient notice of the arrival of a reinforcement to enable them to beat a safe retreat, and we were forced to be content with the amiable individual left in our hands. He did not fail to allude strongly and loudly to their desertion of him, interspersing his remarks with a short extract from their pedigrees, to prove, if he might be credited in his knowledge of their genealogy, that there was in each case a direct canine descent by the mother's side. When I inform the reader that he added considerable point to his observations in the way of sundry expletives, I can leave him to imagine the tenor of the language evoked by the temporary difficulties of this interesting " peasant."

The man was sent, under a sufficient escort, to the house, and I remained behind with Thornton to see what nets there were. The stones placed on the wall of course enabled us to find these. In every instance a sheet net had been used ; and, as there were fourteen altogether, it would appear that a much larger body of poachers must have been there, but it was of course equally evident that they had bolted. Four men could not have watched fourteen nets. Two are quite enough, and even then a hare or rabbit will frequently get at liberty unless the man is very quick, because a sheet net will unroll itself in a few yards. A purse net is of course the safest for a meuse, and yet the poachers frequently use the former kind in preference, as they are so easily set up. A couple of tufts of grass stuck into the wall, and " there you are."

In every instance we found that the marks had been trusted to ; and, as these had been judiciously shifted in the early part of the evening by my wily keeper, it followed as a matter of course that the net had been set against the *blank wall :* and the poachers would thus have had the great satisfaction of hearing the hares come through, about four or five yards from where the net was !

There was no further incident connected with our prisoner, more than that he was utterly unknown to any of our party when we came to make a candlelight investigation of his lineaments. His expressive countenance dwelt not in the recollection of Oakes, or even of the three under-keepers who had assisted us, and the prisoner himself, with a possible determination to keep his present predicament a future secret from his " doating wife and helpless little ones "— that's the proper cant, I believe—declined to throw any light upon his name, or upon the locality that had the inestimable blessing of calling him a denizen.

We read in books on natural history that the captive gazelle and gentle turtle-dove, torn from their home in the wild prairie or the grove rendered impervious to the midday rays of the scorching sun, refuse all comfort, and pine away and languishingly die when imprisoned by the ruthless hand of man. Would that I were able to apply this beautiful analogy to the subject of my narrative ! I regret to say that the very reverse of all this was the case ; for we had no sooner ensconced him in a seat by the kitchen fire than he

addressed me (with a familiarity utterly unjustified by long
acquaintance) in the following marked words : " I say, Gaffer, if
you've got a bit o' grub and a drain o' beer, I'll put it out o' sight
for yer in quick sticks ! "

All sentiment after this was, of course, out of place, and, ordering
the creature comforts in question to be produced for the joint
sustenance of the keepers and their prisoner, I marched off to bed.
Having to go as far as the bath-room for a bootjack, I now take
upon myself to say that the smell of tobacco-smoke plainly perceptible
up the back stairs was much stronger than could have been created
by one performer on that beautiful instrument, the " short pipe."
Can it be that that confounded impudent scoundrel who called me
" Gaffer " is coolly smoking with my keepers ? Shall I go down
and put his pipe out ? No ! I will not disturb him. " Little he'll
reck if I let him smoke on."

One of the servants knocked at the door of my bedroom soon after
daybreak, and said that Thornton was waiting below stairs. I went
down to him, and he asked whether I would like to walk as far as
the plantation, and inspect by daylight the effect of his having
removed the poachers' marks. I agreed to do so, and off we started.

As previously stated, we had found all the nets the night before ;
and so far as their displacement was likely to be owing to hares
knocking them down, there they might have stood for a century.
Every one had been spread against the blank wall, as was evident
enough by the tufts of grass, some of which were lying on the
ground, and some still sticking in the wall. A hearty burst of British
laughter on *my* part greeted the discovery. Thornton, like a good-
disciplined soldier, smiled a grave smile, but I am sure he must
have been " in fits," as I was, had he been alone.

It is very probable that, had the poachers used " purse nets," they
would have discovered the deception immediately ; but had they
done so they could have had no sport that night, for it does not do
to have to hunt about and find meuses in the night-time, especially
when *imitations* (which, on a tolerably *light* night, would not be distinguishable from real ones) have been instituted.

The poachers had completely fallen into a trap as regards that *bleating*. It is a very common arrangement with these gentry, if they mean to make a stand, to collect on an alarm-post previously arranged, and then, if their pluck or numbers will carry them through, to attack the keepers in combined strength. If their rendezvous should be accidentally occupied by the keepers, they improvise any field that may be handy, and then commence bleating ; and this signal is generally sure to bring up their reinforcements. The plan succeeded admirably as far as we were concerned; and had not Morton adopted it (on speculation), we should most certainly have had to remain content with a capture of nets only.

The fellow whom we had caught was very much disposed at one time to give us the names of his associates. He entered very fully into the history of the expedition, and got into such a " wax " about the retreat of his friends to the (doubtless) duet of " The butty I left behind me," that he nearly let slip their "names and rank," but he checked himself in time. I heard all this from Thornton, who, with the other keepers, had, as previously related, sat up listening to these "Extracts from the Diary and Times of a celebrated Poacher."

The conviction of our prisoner followed in due course, and he was consigned to the county gaol without a fine, as it was a case of night poaching. In strictness it was " night poaching with violence," the only difference being that the violence was exercised by the poacher's friends on his own precious skull, and, from what Morton told me, I am only surprised at his surviving the attack he received. Had I been on the spot and witnessed it, I would have bet " two to one on the ' striker' " with anyone who felt disposed to take me.

Things went smoothly on without much variety ; our game increased steadily, and I found myself in a couple of years in a situation to return the civility of my neighbours by asking them to *battues* equal to their own. I will not, however, inflict the details of any of these gatherings upon my readers. One *battue* is the same as another, generally speaking, just as one tiger hunt in India is the same as another ; and the latter subject has been worn threadbare

M

enough, goodness knows. I shall, therefore, carry the reader through the autumn and winter, emerging in the pleasant month of May, and relate a very humorous circumstance that occurred about the 15th of that month.

I think I have omitted to mention the fact (and, after all, it is a very trifling one) that I had been at considerable pains to encourage the rooks to build in some good-sized elm and ash trees at the back of the stable. I procured some old rook nests from a neighbour the very first year I arrived, and caused them to be tied with strong cord into the likeliest-looking forks I could discern at the tops of these trees. The result was that a couple of rooks had commenced building, and pulled first one nest, and then the others, all to pieces; but the sticks being, I suppose, " past their best," they had rejected them all, and set to work in a business-like way with new and proper materials. Ten days after their commencing four more pair came, then four more, and the consequence was, that I had nine pair of rooks regularly settled.

I need not say that I watched their progress with very great satisfaction, and, as it was so small a colony, I never dreamt of their attracting the attention of professed rook stealers. I was, however, mistaken, as the sequel will show.

Two of the nests were built in the top of a very high Scotch fir, possessing an extremely thick and bushy head. I was sitting in my library on the evening of the 15th, and had, in fact, arrived at the conclusion that it was getting on to bedtime, when I heard the rooks suddenly commence a great disturbance. I ran round to the yard, and could distinctly see the whole flock flying about at no great height, and making such a noise as persuaded me there must be something wrong. I looked at the trees, and they appeared to contain no other burden than the rooks' nest, and yet the tenants of them would not be pacified. I then went into the yard and knocked up my gardener, who quickly dressed and came out. My head groom, a very humorous fellow, who had been a rough rider in the Bays, and whose name was Currey, joined us; and still after a close inspection we seemed no wiser.

Suddenly Ourrey said, "I'll fetch the gun," and he disappeared for a few moments and returned with a stable-fork in his hand, shouting out, "I can see yer, yer blackguard; come down, or I'll soon fetch yer with a charge of shot." To my intense amazement, a voice screamed out from the top of the Scotch fir, "Don't shoot, don't shoot, and I'll come down!" In another instant down came the body to which the voice belonged, and fell a prisoner into our hands. He turned out to be a big lad of about seventeen, and a terrible fright he was in. He excused himself by saying, when he could find words to express himself clearly, that he was taking a message to Colonel Chambers; whereupon Ourrey dumbfounded him by requesting to know "Whether Colonel Chambers lived up that tree?" The lad had not touched a single young rook, for, luckily, he had heard my house door open immediately on arriving at the top of the tree, and the rooks had not actually been aware of his presence till that moment also.

I let him go quits for the fright, and took care the next day to rear a ladder and hammer tenter-hooks into the trees a long way up, and where there happened to be no boughs whereon to rest and extract them.

Although I have made this incident appear as a modern occurrence, it actually happened some years ago; and should it meet the eye of Ourrey, of the Bays, I make no doubt he will remember the laugh we had against the rook stealer by his very apposite question.

Reader, the "Experiences" are now finished. Messrs. Thornton, Oakes, and Oo. must henceforth carry on their occupation unnoticed, as far as I am concerned; and if in the relation of all our adventures I have afforded amusement and combined instruction with it, it will be a very pleasing circumstance for reflection.

Printed by Horace Cox, 346, Strand, London, W.C.

CPSIA information can be obtained
at www.ICGtesting.com
Printed in the USA
LVHW080415210220
647652LV00017BA/235